# The Marriage Map

# The Marriage Map
## The Road to Transforming Your Marriage From Ordeal to Adventure

By
**Barbara R. Grossman, Ph.D.**
**& Michael J. Grossman, M.D.**

SILVER TORCH PRESS
SELF IMPROVEMENT, BUSINESS DEVELOPMENT BOOKS AND MAGAZINES

The Marriage Map: The Road to Transforming Your Marriage from Ordeal to Adventure ©2018 by Barbara R. Grossman, Ph.D. & Michael J. Grossman, M.D.

Printed in the United States of America.

Cover design by Michael De Hoyos, Jr.

ISBN: 978-1-942707-80-6
Library of Congress Control Number: 2018938311

 Published by Silver Torch Press
www.SilverTorchPress.com
Jill@SilverTorchPress.com

Information provided in this book is for informational purposes only. This information is NOT intended as a substitute for the advice provided by your mental health or other healthcare professional, or any information contained on or in any product. All matters regarding your mental, emotional, and physical health require medical supervision. Neither the author nor the publisher shall be liable or responsible for any loss or damage allegedly arising from any information or suggestion in this book.

# Acknowledgements

The actual writing of our book arises out of our 25 years of experience in conducting marriage classes. We are extremely grateful for the editing support from Professor Pianta, San Diego Mesa College, our dear friend Bruce Giddens, Jeff Russell and his Christian publishing group, and Jill Fagan and Gwen Weiler of Silver Torch Press.

# Dr. Barbara

My mentors have been many: Dr. Howard Clinebell, Ph.D., the grandfather of Protestant pastoral counseling and my clinical supervisor; George Markham MFT, M.Div., Baptist minister and director of St. Joseph Hospital's pastoral counseling program; Stanley Krippner, Ph.D., my dear college professor and world-famous humanistic psychologist who introduced me to the world of creative people; The Rev. Terry Cole-Whittaker taught me how to put faith into action; James Fowler, Ph.D., who taught me to apply structural development theory to the development of faith; Dr. James Sanders, Ph.D., renowned Dead Sea Scrolls scholar who taught me how to understand religious texts existentially; Dr. Robert Kegan, Ph.D., Harvard professor and author whose books and conversations inspired us to create our spiral map; and our dear friend Jack Rafferty, who taught us how to be a happy, romantic couple.

# Dr. Michael

I am so grateful that while I was busy conquering my space, my wife brought all of her mentors into my life and I learned that I too can reach into others and nurture. In addition, we are grateful to our Rabbi, Zalman Marcus, of Chabad Mission Viejo who brings to life the Hasidic tradition of the Lubavitcher Rebbe. He provides a home for our spiritual path.

# Table of Contents

# Preface

## By Michael

A king without a queen, the Zohar says, is neither great nor a king. For it is the woman who empowers the man to conquer his space.

And it is the man who empowers the woman to penetrate and nurture hers.

And then the man will learn from this woman that he, too, can reach within others and provide nurture. And the woman will learn that she, too, can conquer."

Rabbi Menachem Mendel Schneerson
The Seventh Lubavitcher Rebbe, Sabbath talk, 1991

Marriage is very different today than it was a hundred years ago. The roles of husband and wife are more unclear, and our society seems to have no set rules for them. Even so, most people have great expectations for romantic satisfaction within marriage, as well as high hopes for healing and personal development. Each partner yearns, consciously or unconsciously, for the other to heal their early childhood wounds, and to love, accept, and cherish them.

The marriage journey is a hero's and heroine's journey with many adventures including the experience of facing your fears, finding courage, discovering mentors, learning new skills, and dying to your old sense of self which feels something like depression before it feels like a new and more vital life. It will take time to go on this adventure, but it is a worthy human endeavor. It promises to transform your experience of love into something much more intense than you could ever imagine.

As you read the pages of this book, you will notice that Barbara and I have openly shared the experiences of our marriage— the difficult episodes and life transitions that are inevitable in most relationships. Understanding our process for encountering and resolving those experiences in the context of adult development will allow you to reflect on your own life and inspire you to use the challenges in your marriage for improvement and growth in your romantic relationship.

The story that leads to our classes and this book began in our early thirties when, late one night, a rare Southern California thunderstorm approached our neighborhood. Barbara had been pressing me to talk about some emotional difficulty in our marriage while I was impatient to get to sleep. Yet the more she pressured me, the angrier I became. I was exhausted from work and was desperate to relax and get to sleep. Every few minutes, a distant flash of lightning flickered in our bedroom. A few seconds after that, some muffled thunder growled. Barbara insisted that I was uncooperative, unreasonable, and unwilling to talk about the issues, but I kept putting her off by saying that I was tired and to wait until tomorrow after we had gotten some sleep. Still, she persisted, and we both became angrier.

Barbara kept insisting, until finally we both exploded. I yelled, "You are so selfish," to which she screamed back, "You don't care about me!"

Just then, in the middle of our yelling and screaming, a bolt of lightning shook the house with a deafening boom! The huge flash lit up our bedroom like daylight for a moment and showered fiery sparks through the protective metal grating around the fireplace. A message from the heavens? We were stunned into silence and just looked at each other, suddenly realizing the destructive power of our anger.

Right then and there, we both knew we needed to find a better way to communicate and work out our individual emotional needs.

In every marriage, there are issues that create the same fight over and over again. The fight may take different forms and appear in different situations, but it remains the same conflict at the core. Think about your own marriage and your repeated patterns of unhappiness. A deep commitment to resolve those underlying issues in marriage requires each husband and wife to undertake a healing journey as an individual, and a combined healing journey as partners.

The process of healing my marriage with Barbara required me to learn new skills and acquire new abilities, all of which seemed overwhelming at first. Listening to my wife was something I had to learn to do—even if it was painful.

I have a vivid memory of sitting in a communication training class and pairing off with a random student. I had to listen to my classmate and offer feedback about not only what she said, but also what I thought about her underlying feelings. I was pretty good at paraphrasing what my classmate said, but I had no clue about her underlying feelings. Even with a helpful list of words to describe her emotions, I failed. It was only then that I realized I needed to grow in this emotional realm of life.

The hero's journey is somewhat different for a man and a woman. After a man learns competence, he needs to learn humility. After a woman learns connection, she needs to find her voice. The path of the hero and heroine is not supposed to be a smooth ride. There are no shortcuts. Seeing the world, yourself, and your partner from a bigger perspective is always an intense process of stretching and letting go.

The idea that something should not be happening to us on this journey or that we don't deserve this emotional pain comes from that part of us that strives to preserve our ego's limited perspective. This attitude blocks progress on the healing journey. From our point of view as a selfish, self-centered egocentric being, we are constantly being shortchanged, cheated, mistreated, and not valued as highly as we expect. From a bigger perspective, as God might look at us, we need to be worked on, cracked, molded, and transformed into a wise and loving being.

In the following pages, we provide a road map for a lifetime of relationship growth.

In our companion workbook, *Falling In Love Forever: 3 Keys to a Fulfilling Romantic Partnership*, we provide three key practices and principles that form the basic skill set for navigating through the journey of marriage. Those key practices can be used throughout the lifetime of marriage, much like the skills of throwing and catching in baseball or holding a firm but flexible frame in ballroom dancing.

The emotional and cognitive development that is stimulated by the conflicts of two personalities in partnership and the simultaneous desire for love and family is both intense and rewarding. It is the catalyst for healing and deepening love. Our purpose is to support your journey so that you fulfill the potential of your marriage.

Best wishes for love,
Michael Grossman

# Introduction

## By Barbara

For our first 10 years, Michael and I had a pleasant marriage. As the husband, Michael set the direction and goals. As the wife, I supported those goals, and Michael was very happy and comfortable. After our two daughters entered pre-school, I went back to graduate school to develop myself professionally and personally. That was when we became two people with our own points of view, and life became much more difficult.

Now, many years later, we tell our story because it offers hope to couples who find themselves trapped in similar patterns of isolation. It is so painful to experience the promise of love turning into disappointment after the first years of marriage. For us, it was a highly personal but very predictable experience. When we step back and view ourselves as a couple, it's clear that I felt neglected and ignored as a wife and young mother while Michael focused on his career and personal development. I found Michael distant and self-centered because of the time he spent away from the family. My attempts at creating a closer connection often ended in frustration and anger. This only aggravated the problem because, when Michael experienced my anger, he would only withdraw more.

We saw many therapists and teachers, and we attended programs for self-development in those days. Thanks to them, we learned the tools to re-create ourselves and our marriage. It helped that I worked independently to establish my own identity and self-respect. Women who marry young often lose their sense

1

of self during the childbearing years. It also helped that Michael was willing to stretch and grow emotionally. For all our advanced professional education, when it came to the most intimate aspects of our lives, we were like most couples, struggling to learn how to deal effectively with uncomfortable emotions. Our journey was challenging. It took years for us to accomplish our goal.

## Romantic Marriage is, by its Nature, a Personal Growth Process

Joseph Campbell, perhaps the most famous mythologist of the twentieth century, wrote of the modern and romantic model, "Marriage is not a love affair; it is an ordeal." But did he mean an ordeal in the sense of relentless struggle and deprivation? No. He was referring to a trial that, although involving great effort and sacrifice, would always lead to personal transformation if navigated successfully. In that sense, you can compare the ordeal of marriage to the chemist's crucible.

A crucible is a container unaffected by extremely high temperatures, in which two metals will melt and join to form an alloy. Chemists and metallurgists use crucibles to create alloys that will be superior in one way or another to either of the two starting metals. Often, the process results in impurities that separate out of the pure alloy and float to the top. This is like married life, because two previously separate individuals unite as intimately as possible to become something greater than either was originally. The promise of emotional, spiritual, and physical intimacy in a marriage becomes real only if the partners can endure the intense heat that is natural to a romantic relationship.

In a marriage, the heat of the crucible is romantic love and passion, as well as the pressures of everyday life and the expectations we brought to the relationship. The impurities that rise to the top of the alloy in the crucible are like the resentments, grudges, fears, and complaints that get in the way of a loving relationship. However, a relationship that is conscious and growing can sort those out and resolve them. We believe that the chemical process of heating two metals to become something stronger and purer than either of the starting materials is a model and metaphor for the possibilities of married life. The process of a marriage can transform two individuals into a more sublime, joyful union.

Having taught these principles to thousands of couples, we have seen couples view their marriages in a new light. They understand that obstacles are not insurmountable barriers, but are rather opportunities to go deeper into the experience of forging a strong and healthy marriage. Learning the processes for navigating a relationship when the temperature is hot (or cold) makes all the difference.

The crucible is a powerful metaphor, for it symbolizes the melding not only of the two partners in a marriage, but also the merging of romantic love and married life. It can be easy to maintain a romantic relationship when you don't have to deal with the practicalities of life. Similarly, married life without romance can also be easy to maintain. That is why the model of traditional arranged marriage, where the finances and common culture of the extended families exerted such an influence, has endured for so long.

We were about forty years old when we realized that we had reached a new point of satisfaction in our marriage, and we began to teach a workshop that provided couples easier ways to experience what we had struggled so long to learn. Since then, we have taught several thousand couples how to develop the practical tools that can transform their marriages from a struggle to a new kind of joy.

Michael and I bring different perspectives and skill sets to our classes. With a Ph.D. in theology and personality, my background is in psychology and theology. Michael was a board-certified family physician for thirty-five years. He now specializes in anti-aging and regenerative medicine. He has also taught meditation techniques to thousands of people over the last 30 years, helping them to integrate spiritual experiences into their everyday lives. Our two unique backgrounds draw on the best of both the Western and Eastern understanding of the body, mind, and spirit, and we draw heavily on that expertise in each of our classes. Thousands of our course participants have tested the concepts in our classes over the years. We have been moved by seeing husbands and wives rediscovering their love for each other after years of resentment, learning to talk to each other about what really matters, understanding each other's wounds, and providing real emotional support for each other.

The desire to share our healing journey of married life, and inspire others to learn how to develop the practical tools to likewise travel that path, motivated us to write this book.

In Part 1, without getting too academic, we are going to introduce to you a particular map of development. The map will help you understand how a personality evolves over a lifetime. It helps to explain the discomfort that often grows between partners who once were harmonious.

In Parts 2 and 3, we illustrate that map by sharing our own stories that chronicle those stages of development. We will each describe our personal journey, as we trust that you will see yourself and your partner in our challenges and dilemmas. We also will incorporate archetypal stories from our Western culture that remarkably parallel our own stories. We believe there is a framework of development in Western civilization in myth and story that reveals a healing journey in the path to intimate partnership. In doing so, we seek to personalize this process of self-development and individuation in marriage in a way that we believe will inspire you to grow into a greater reality of love, acceptance, and partnership.

It's our sincere hope that by sharing these principles and experiences, you'll be guided through your own rough patches and not hastily conclude that your relationship is fatally flawed or hopeless.

Once you see the big vision of the potential of personal and partnership growth inherent in marriage, we invite you to take our *Falling in Love Forever* classes to learn the specific skills which will allow you to support each other as you grow though this journey.

Wishing you love,
Barbara Grossman

# Part 1

## The Map of Individual Development

# Chapter 1

# Psycho-Spiritual Stages

Developmental psychologists since the pioneering Jean Piaget have tried to understand what pushes an individual toward either autonomy or attachment. The interplay of those two needs profoundly affects an individual's way of being and knowing. Life is dynamic. We change, and as we change, the way we construct the world around us also changes. All of this has enormous implications for relationships.

Perhaps one of you concentrates on self and seems detached, while the other partner is more comfortable in a belonging frame of mind. Or you may both be growing into a focus on the self, but with a sense of living parallel lives and a dwindling connection. Each of those patterns can create the experience of growing apart. Such an experience is predictable, but fortunately it can be temporary and manageable if the two of you are conscious and reflective about your development, and each takes responsibility for directing his or her own development.

The dynamics of autonomy and attachment evolve through different stages over a lifetime, and unique values characterize each stage. Each stage builds upon the previous ones, alternating in emphasis on autonomy or attachment. We can visualize these stages as the path of a helix.

At each stage, one organizes the experience of one's self and life in a different way. Each has its own logic and builds on the prior states. Subsequent stages provide more differentiation of

## Psycho-Spiritual Stages

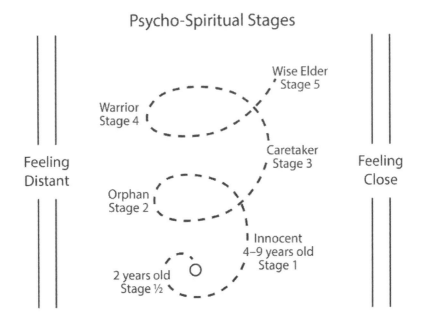

self. Note the pattern that stands out (see diagram). At some times in your life, you feel close to the people you love, and at other times you feel distant. Naturally, the same holds true for your partner. Unfortunately, those times may not coincide in a harmonious way.

You feel close in the stage of "innocence," from the ages of about four to ten years old, again as an adult "caretaker" in stage three, from the ages of about twenty to thirty-odd years old, and yet again as a "wise elder," if you become one, at the age of about fifty years old or older. You feel distant as a two-year-old when you learn how to say "no" (hence the term "terrible twos"), again as "orphan" while in your teens when you feel disappointed in your parents and detach from them, and yet again as an adult "warrior" when you pursue your dreams.

The diagram of the helix represents the moving back and forth in a lifelong tension between autonomy and attachment. Each stage has its strengths and its weaknesses. Internalized moral values and concern for the good of others are generally present starting in stage three (caretaker). From that point on, we believe that it is inappropriate to automatically identify persons in the later stages as better people. The later stages do not necessarily indicate a higher morality, although they can solve more of life's challenges.

Understand each stage, then, as an evolutionary resting place that resolves the tensions of individuality and attachment. Each succeeding stage gives you a greater sense of self, with more skills to solve life's problems. Each stage also gives you a new perspective by which to organize your perception and experience of your self.

Now we will briefly describe stages zero to five. As you follow along, think of how each stage applies in your own life experience, and then how it applies in your partner's. Later, you will fill in a chart as you reflect on your own stages of development and compare it to the one your partner completed. You may reflect together on the difficult transition from caretaker to warrior if you have experienced it.

Each person moves from one stage to another gradually, usually over a period of years. Try to identify the stages you have already passed through and where you are now. Stages beyond your present stage will appear abstract and difficult to understand. You know that you are changing from one stage to another when life presents you with challenges that your earlier ways of thinking and behaving cannot resolve, and you respond by stretching yourself. Being in a stage is generally comfortable, but transitioning to a new stage is usually not comfortable.

## *Stage Zero: Unity with Mother*

Your human journey started in childhood with a kind of unified experience with your mother. It lasted four to six months.

Then you began to see your mother as separate from yourself, but you had no idea that your mother had needs of her own as a person separate from you. You began to struggle with having your needs met, as your mother didn't seem willing to do everything that you wanted. So, you then went through a period of separation and lost your previous intimacy with your mother. We call that stage one-half, or the terrible twos.

## Stage One: The Innocent

The pendulum swung back to feeling a sense of intimacy and closeness through your early childhood years, until the ages of about eight or ten. You felt a part of your family. You felt close and comfortable with your role among the other members of your family. It was a big movement and journey from that earlier stage in which you saw everything as revolving around you. We call such a child an "innocent."

## Stage Two: The Orphan

The next journey moved away from the intimacy of your family to find close friends in your teenage years. You had relationships in which you helped and enjoyed your friends, and they helped and enjoyed you in return. At that stage, you were your needs and desires. "I'll scratch your back, if you'll scratch mine" was the mode of being. Some psychologists call this stage the "orphan." We also know that many individuals in this stage eventually enter a transition phase that we call the "wanderer." As wanderers, they search for values and ideals to guide their lives.

## Stage Three: The Caretaker

Most individuals eventually go on to the next journey, where you become involved in your own family. Here, you once again join closely with others and feel connected to others when you create a marriage and have children. Connections at this stage often include a community of faith. In this stage, you become your marriage and other relationships. Although you recognize that you have desires, you are not those desires as you were when you were in stage two. At this stage of life, you struggle to communicate with your loved ones. You try to balance your desires with theirs as you feel a deep connection with your family. You feel that you are your family. We call such an adult a "caretaker."

## *Stage Four: The Warrior*

Not all take this journey, which is again one of separation from loved ones. At this stage, you have your own point of view and your own beliefs, principles, and ideals. Your struggle is to allow others to have their points of view. At this stage, you are your principles and beliefs. You have your marriage and other relationships, and work on those relationships. Yet you have a sense of distance from your loved ones. The amount of separation depends upon their beliefs and principles, which may be different from yours. You concentrate on your purpose and goals. We call such an adult a "warrior."

## *Stage Five: The Wise Elder*

Only a few take this journey. It again brings you close to your loved ones. It develops your capacity for intimacy and expression of feelings. You come to an appreciation of paradox, symbols, rituals, and the ambiguity of eternal truths. You experience that you are your individuality. You have principles and work on them, but also have a sense of having transcended them.

This stage reflects those prior, when as a caretaker you were no longer your desires, although you had desires. Likewise, as a warrior you have your marriage and other relationships but no longer have your sense of self defined by relationship. The prior stages helped you develop a strong ego, your personal sense of self. Stage five allows the ego to become a transparent container through which to express your soul. That is a self larger than your personality. We call such an adult "a wise elder."

The predominant upsets in modern marriages are the result of transitions out of the caretaker and into the warrior stages. Those transitions occur at different times for men and women. This book starts with a quotation from the Rebbe because he succinctly makes our point: The journey of a man and a woman involves a different timetable for particular lessons in development. At first, the masculine conquers his world through competency. Usually, the feminine first nurtures and penetrates her world through emotional connection. Ultimately, men and women need to gain the integration to both conquer and nurture, but typically they do this in a different sequence.

However, moving through these stages can create an earthquake in a marriage. The intensity of the seismic jolt depends on the timing, but it is always uncomfortable. In the next two sections, Part 2 and Part 3, we will share own personal stories in order to illuminate this natural path of adult development.

# Part 2

## Michael's Story

# Chapter 2

# Orphan Stage to Caretaker

## *A Serious Illness and an Epiphany*

I was a happy enough kid growing up. I liked sports and was very good in school. My family had good times together, especially in the summers. When I was 13 years old, however, I began a two-year bout with hepatitis that changed my life and forced me to withdraw from sports and active living. All I could do was go to school and come home. I changed from a teenager living for the moment to an introspective young person. I no longer was the jokester who teased others. Rather, I felt separate from others as I could not participate in their activities. I felt cheated for having to miss so much of life as a young teen. Sickness and disease seemed unfair, and something to fight against.

The experience caused me to think about life and death, even after I recovered. By then, I knew that school and sports were not all there was to life. When I started college, as a 16-year-old, I was on a full-fledged quest to find answers to life's deep philosophical questions: What is the meaning of life? Is there a God? Even when I took physics courses, I found spiritual issues embedded in scientific concepts. As a pre-med student, I majored in chemistry and minored in philosophy. My mind enjoyed scientific and spiritual challenges.

My family did not appreciate this kind of idealism. My parents were honest and practical people. When I was 19, I told my mother that I was moving out to explore my quest. She did not want to hear about my quest, and I felt hurt and disappointed. She did not understand my thirst for knowledge of life's deepest purpose.

My parents stopped their financial support. I lost my car; my college payments were my own. I felt like an orphan, abandoned and disowned. But at the same time, I was exhilarated. I was living independently, freed from the restrictions of my family's rules and regulations of where and when I could do things. I was free to pursue my quest for knowledge.

My mother would not have appreciated the insight I gained while walking on the hilly, cobblestone streets of the Bronx as a college student, anxious about the meaning of life. I read the existentialist French philosophers Sartre and Camus, who postulated that there was no meaning to life or death. The existentialists believed the physical world existed, but it had no inherent meaning. According to them, this meaninglessness should create dread. And it did for me, constantly, for many months. One morning on the walk to school up a tree-lined path, I felt Sartre's

existential nausea. I cried out inside: "If there is a God, please hear me. Please show me a way to see life differently."

I took a deep breath and opened my eyes, and a maple tree inexplicably drew my attention. Looking at the tree, little pieces of silver metal sticking out of its trunk in random places bewildered me. How could metal be growing out of a maple tree? My mind was quiet as I circled the tree. The metal seemed to be growing out all around the trunk, but generally in a vertical pattern.

Suddenly, I realized that the metal was a remnant of a fence that someone put around the tree to support and protect it. Eureka! Over the years, the tree trunk had grown and now practically engulfed the entire fence. I saw it as a metaphor. Instead of fighting the fence put there to protect it, the tree simply grew beyond that limitation by accepting the fence as part of itself. When I saw this in that way, and realized the possibility of accepting and transcending the limitations of my life, I felt flooded with peace. I needed to stop resisting death and surrender my win-lose mentality that was causing me so much bitterness. Allowing death to be a part of life opened my awareness to a bigger, transcendent world beyond physical limitations.

That encounter with the maple tree continues to inspire and teach me. It teaches me not to fight or be resentful about life's limitations. Simply allowing something to be, without resisting it, can be transformative. I try to see the good intentions in limitations; the original iron fence protected the young tree. Protection can look like limitation and restriction when we are maturing. Yet, the tree's example of embracing the restriction and continuing to grow illustrates the course that has brought me surprising satisfaction.

Looking back, the metaphor of the maple tree helped me to emotionally and intellectually accept death as a part of life. It seems that by giving up a fighting mentality, I opened my mind to a deeper reality of an inherent intelligence in life from a transcendent source, which softened the tightness in my abdomen that had been draining my energy and enthusiasm for life. This acceptance of limitation and/or death gave me energy and direction in my quest to find meaning and purpose in life. Soon I began to pursue meditation as a possible way to connect with this transcendence.

Sometimes fighting is needed and gives us energy. But often accepting and letting go allows us to transform ourselves into the next stage of life. This can mistakenly feel like giving in to the thing we are resisting (i.e. the fence or dying). However, if we are so busy resisting our old hurts and resentments and physical limitations, we may miss the bigger view of life which is waiting for us.

The tree and fence metaphor lives as a way to deal with how growth feels in many places along life's journey.

## *The Early Marriage Years: All about Me*

I met Barbara just before graduating from college, when I was just beginning to explore meditation. She was a good listener, and interested in the same questions as I about the purpose of life. She was willing to hear my perceptions of life, and read and discuss my favorite books. We first developed a relationship as friends. There was a month I was away on a meditation course, and we wrote letters to each other about my ideas and her responses to Hermann Hesse's books *Siddhartha* and *Narcissus and Goldmund*, which were popular at that time. Our conversations were always pleasant, interesting, and stimulating.

Meditation gave me a peaceful space, a map of the universe, and a method for growth. I had a wise teacher and a community that valued spirituality, and I was very satisfied. One of the only requests I remember making to Barbara was that she learn to meditate, which was not her natural inclination. But she did it for me, and I was pleased. That completed the package. I was happy to marry her.

During the next few years, I immersed myself in professional training. Meditation courses were a welcome respite. I loved the experiences of meditation and the knowledge that came with it. Before long, I finished my medical training. Barbara was pregnant, and we planned to take a year off to live in the meditation community. We packed up our apartment, put our belongings into storage, and went to Switzerland. Four months later, Barbara wanted to leave and make a home for our baby. I did not understand her thinking and did not want to leave, so we decided to ask our meditation teacher for his direction.

## Learning to Value the Feminine

I loved participating in the meditation course. It was such a breath of fresh air after the rat race and exhaustion of my medical internship. I thought that I could easily earn money later as a physician to pay back all the loans we owed. Yes, my wife was having a baby in a few months, but we could have the baby here in Europe and stay in this comfortable course, with food and rooms provided while we experienced the pleasure of spiritual growth.

Barbara, on the other hand, felt trapped by the schedule of meditation, yoga, breathing exercises, meetings, meals, and back to meditation. She wanted to go home, and seemed to be behaving irrationally. I thought that I was good in tolerating her, but she frequently leaned on my commitment to meditation to keep her on track. So, I agreed to ask our meditation teacher whether we should stay or go home. I just knew that the teacher, in his wisdom, would advise us to stay. He had been telling everyone to borrow money, put off projects, just do whatever it took to stay for six months and realize the full value of this advanced course.

It was difficult to see the teacher. With about 3,000 students in the course, there usually was a long line to see him, and many attempts to do so resulted only in disappointment. If we were not able to talk with him, I thought that I could at least tell Barbara that we tried, and then convince her of the wisdom of staying.

When we finally reached the part of the hotel where the teacher was supposed to be, I became confused. Where were the personal guards who protected the teacher from unwanted intruders? Where were the lines of people waiting to get in? My hands were sweating and my heart was racing, but I knew I was right.

Eventually, we arrived at a door, and Barbara uncharacteristically said, "Let's just go in." I hesitated, and then meekly opened the door, expecting someone to shout at me angrily for intruding. But nothing happened. The room was dark. We took our shoes off and quietly sat down on the floor in front of the elevated seat covered with a white sheet.

It took a minute for my eyes to adjust to the barely lit room. A carpet covered the floor. There were just a few people in the room. Wow! The teacher sat on his place of honor with flowers surrounding him. My heart was beating faster. My stomach had butterflies in it. I felt unusually alert. My eyes darted about the room. My ears perked up, listening for any sounds. No one was talking. What was going on?

Barbara nudged me, so I spoke up, "Master, my wife and I were wondering: Would it be better to stay in the course for a few more months as you seem to be suggesting, or should we go home? I think it would be better to stay, since we could easily get loans as I am a doctor. My wife thinks we should go home, as she is seven months pregnant, and worries about money and setting up an actual home."

I was about to continue, but our teacher interrupted me: "Your wife is right! Go home. Be a doctor, make lots of money."

My mind stopped. I felt my world turn upside down as I began to accept this new limitation. I thought about going home and asked, "Should I practice acupuncture and holistic medicine, or be a regular doctor and make more money?" He responded, "Be a regular doctor, make lots of money, but be a better doctor."

There were no more questions in my head, only a whirlpool draining away all my preconceptions about how I was going to live my life. Once outside the door, Barbara was jubilant, jumping up and down like she won a world championship gold medal. Soon, my mind cleared. My life looked different. I had a completely new picture of my life with no doubts about my new direction. Before, I had avoided putting Barbara's feminine desires before my own desires for spiritual growth, but now I had been knighted and given a commission to go into the world and be successful. I saw the path I would take, and now I only had to live into it.

I had much to learn about Barbara. Her desires seemed so unimportant compared to the profundity of my own. She seemed so meek and unassuming, but when she had a desire, something powerful changed in the world to make it happen. The experience with our meditation teacher is just one example of doors opening to fulfill her desires. I had a lot to learn about her feminine nature and feminine power.

By going home, I could no longer avoid the lessons that married life had to teach me. This was a reminder of the lesson I learned from the tree growing around the fence. I could not resist the limitations of married life if I wanted to grow. My logical mind directed me to take a straight path toward spiritual growth. But my path of married life was full of twists and turns, and had surprising developments in store for me. Looking back, I now realize that I was learning that I cannot outsmart life, I cannot outsmart God, and I cannot outsmart life's challenges.

I was now being pushed to be a Warrior who takes on full responsibility for his domain. I needed to set up my own medical practice and support my family, and learn to integrate that with my desire for spiritual enlightenment.

If you had asked me at the time, I would have said my purpose was exclusively to set up my medical practice and become a great medical doctor. But as you will see, my growing edge was in learning in more than just the professional arena.

# Chapter 3

# A Warrior's Growth and Development: Giving up Control, Accepting Life Challenges

A few years later, I learned a lesson about my continued inclination to avoid life's challenges. I was playing a game of dungeons and knights and sorcerers on a Commodore 64 computer with my oldest daughter. We worked hard to strengthen our knights so they could defeat the evil enemy in their evil castle. The game was set up so that if your men died, you had to start over from the beginning and grow the force of your army over a period of many days. There were two ways that men could die: one was in battle, and the other was being caught in a whirlpool. Because I'm such a clever fellow, I quickly learned to fool the computer when our men died by pulling out the plug before the machine could register their deaths. That worked very well, as it allowed our knights to grow ever stronger. The trouble, however, was that we still were not able to defeat the evil sorcerer in the evil castle no matter how powerful our men became.

Six weeks later, in frustration I returned to the store where I had purchased the game, and complained about its faulty programming. After a conversation about what was going on and how I could not defeat the evil sorcerer, the store manager asked what happened when our men fell into the whirlpool and were all drowned. I said, "Of course, I pulled the plug so that I wouldn't lose the strength of my men." The store manager laughed out loud and finally said, "If you had waited three more seconds, you would've seen that all were lost, but then you would wake up in the underworld and have the opportunity to go on a secret adventure to find a special key, which you need to defeat the evil sorcerer."

My cunning and logical mind had outsmarted myself. My linear strategy was brilliant, but I had defeated myself because I was unwilling to give up control. It was yet another metaphor: to achieve my quest, I needed to let my knights go through the whirlpool, just as I needed to risk some loss of control in my life and marriage. I have had to learn that trying to avoid confronting the ordeal of emotional difficulties is counterproductive. Rather, by experiencing feelings and emotional challenges without resisting, I become more open to the deeper dimensions of spiritual growth.

I was married and had started a family. But my vision for my life was focused on personal goals that had very little to do with my marriage. I had a meditation philosophy and method that I believed guaranteed my development. I was now a successful physician and meditation teacher with more than a thousand students.

My natural inclination was to live the linear life strategy that my logical mind had planned out: marriage, children, and career. Meditate and avoid all possible upsets. It was all logical, and I was in control. But it really didn't work. So much so that I now laughingly refer to that as my first marriage to Barbara. My vision was the concept of a young man without as much maturity as he had imagined. Now, I have come to cherish my journey with its exquisite adventures that transcend my logical mind—a journey that has exceeded anything I could ever have imagined.

## Creating Boundaries with Love: Putting My Marriage First

When Barbara went back to graduate school ten years into our marriage, the dynamics of our relationship altered. She began to find her own voice for her needs, desires, and point of view. This was an outgrowth of her training in counseling, and naturally it affected her personally. This was extremely uncomfortable for me, because my point of view had always been the most important in our marriage.

I was about 30 years old then, and Barbara had requested that I define a boundary with my mother so we could balance our time with our two families. As a young husband, I did not know about the importance of boundaries or how to create one. But Barbara helped me, and so that request allowed me to create an adult relationship with my mother. The next time I saw my mother, I explained that I wanted her to agree that, in forthcoming visits from California, Barbara and I would spend less time with her, my father and my brothers, in New York so we could spend more time with Barbara's parents and some of our friends.

"No. I will not agree to it," was my mother's reply. She felt that we didn't see her very often, whereas Barbara's parents traveled to California to visit us "all the time." When we were in New York, my mother said, I should be spending my time with my own family. This went on for about 45 minutes of very heated discussion when, with no resolution in sight, I gave up and said, "Okay. We cannot agree, but I want to give you a hug."

My mother looked at me, puzzled, and wanted to know why I want to give her a hug. I told her that it was because I loved her. That led to a three-minute debate about whether I could give her a hug, because she did not want a hug. But I persisted, and she reluctantly agreed. Then we hugged, and began to cry. Something changed in our relationship after that. My mother had a new respect for me. There was a softness growing in our relationship.

Having a disagreement without anger or resentment is a big deal with anyone—but especially with your mother. Accepting that there can be two valid points of view is a big milestone in personal growth. I disagreed with my mother, but I did not resent her position about our visits. The whole problem dissolved in a way that both brought me closer to my mother and created a healthy independence for me. This occurred as a result of Barbara's request to create clearer boundaries where we defined time to visit her parents on our trips to New York.

## Listening to Your Inner Voice: Yielding to Nurture

At some stages of married life, the struggle between what you want and what your partner wants can represent a considerable dilemma. In my 30's, I still wanted to deepen my spiritual experience by continuing to go on one-to-two week long spiritual retreats. Barbara, however, wanted me at home for the family, not running off, even if it were for a spiritual retreat. My life revolved around my need for time for meditation, work, and lecturing. Having Barbara restrict me in what I could and could not do was oppressive. I am sure that practically all husbands feel that way from time to time, especially when their work or other projects are especially fulfilling.

Barbara felt neglected, but aside from my feeling oppressed by her requests, I was fine. I took Barbara's need for personal time with me to be an intrusion on what I perceived as the real needs of our life. Yet she felt abandoned, ignored, and unimportant. For her, the value of intimacy, sharing, and family and personal time spent together was the critical value of our marriage relationship.

Then, while attending a medical workshop on imagery as a transformational tool, I had an experience that changed the way I perceived my struggles with Barbara. I was asked to deal with a personal problem by calling up images to my mind, images that would represent the problem. I conjured a vine wrapping itself around my ankles and pulling me down to earth, holding me and trapping me there. I was frantically trying to get away from the vine, but unable to pry myself loose. At that point, the instructions for the exercise called on me to talk to the image symbolizing the problem.

I imagined speaking to the vine: "What do you want from me? Why hold me down? I cannot move."

"I want you to be close to me," the vine said.

I answered, "I cannot be close to you. I need to go my way. I have things to do to reach my dreams and goals, and I can't let you hold me in your grasp." Then the vine asked, "Where do you have to go, and what do you have to do?"

I said, "I have to be spiritually alive to give out knowledge, to

28

mentor people, and do my lecturing, writing, and meditation."

The vine replied, "I can help you. I can create a shelter in the forest. It will be a beautiful, covered, spiritual retreat, structured by my vines. You could live in it and be creative, hold classes, be a teacher and mentor, and you can be close to me while I support your dreams and goals."

Then the vine morphed into a beautiful shelter, with the vines forming a spiritual retreat in the forest. There I could see students coming inside and studying. In that forest abode, I was able to give spiritual knowledge while feeling nurtured and supported by the vines. It was an extremely fulfilling vision that warmed my heart.

In marriage, men usually focus on their goals to accomplish through work, while women typically focus on the relationship. According to Barbara, in the first part of our marriage I was over-intellectualized and not open to a deep emotional connection with her. I held my spiritual values very cerebrally, pushing away the deep feelings of my heart because they did not conform to my rational and logical worldview.

Through that imagery exercise, I imagined not resisting Barbara's request to be emotionally closer. I saw a more fulfilling vision of possibilities, and that provided a new framework for accepting Barbara's desire to hold me close.

Seeing the validity of Barbara's point of view helped me to mature, and it moved me on a path that was less rigid and more loving. The restrictions that I imagined Barbara placing on me were, in fact, an opportunity to expand my perspective and to grow beyond the limitations I had placed on myself. I saw the opportunity for each of us to realize our dreams by working together.

Sometime later, Barbara told me that although I thought I was being a good father, I was actually an absent father. I was so busy with my work that I really had no time for my children. Fortunately, by that time I had become open to different points of view about my life and work commitments. I began regularly spending time with my two girls, who were about six and seven years old then. We played at sports, took bicycle rides, and played games together. Enjoying more activities as a family had a profound effect on my relationships with Barbara and our daughters.

## *Learning Humility*

Growing in confidence and achievement through one's career is a big part of most men's lives. Not surprisingly then, successful men frequently struggle with pride and haughtiness. For a man, vulnerability and sensitivity to feelings can seem like a weakness. As a result, many men need to learn lessons of humility. Personally, in my 30's, I had not yet learned that lesson.

Now I can see how I acted superior to other people. I was interested in meditation and spiritual growth, so I naturally felt I was a step above. Feeling superior to others was a way to distance myself from them. While many experiences helped me remove that obstacle to intimacy with others, this next example surprised me in a dramatic way. I had no idea I could be so arrogant. I was blind to what God wanted from me: to be humble with others.

For Rosh Hashanah, the Jewish New Year, more than 900 people would gather at our synagogue to pray and ask God for forgiveness. Most never came to synagogue at any other time than these high holy days—unlike me, who enjoyed going every week. During prayers that continue through the entire day, I would often sit with my eyes closed, deep in meditation and great peace. I felt that God enjoyed my deep peaceful awareness, which brought me closer to Him. In one of these moments, I had the thought that God would rather people genuinely pray and meditate like me, instead of reciting singsong, third-grade responsive readings in English, which was what most of those other people were only capable of doing.

Suddenly, a searing pain pierced my temples. I thought I had burst a blood vessel in my head and was dying. Ten seconds passed. I was not dead, but the pain was as strong as ever. I panicked, wondered what had happened. What happened, I soon realized, was that, contrary to my thought, maybe God does want to hear those prayers! I prayed silently: "I take back that previous thought. God does want to hear their prayers. God loves their third-grade, singsong prayers." And immediately the excruciating pain in my temples vanished.

Never again would I judge anyone's prayers to God. I no longer imagined I could judge anyone's spiritual state of growth. Their relationship to God is beyond my ability to evaluate. I gained a lot from this experience. I no longer looked down my nose at other people's spiritual state. I became less self-righteous with Barbara as I increased my acceptance of her own process of growth. I no longer thought I had an exclusive perspective on what God wants from us. This was one more of many life adventures that helped me learn to appreciate what it means to let others into my heart.

### *Learning to Receive*

A big lesson in my maturation was learning to receive love. I used to be so busy caring for others and trying to satisfy my need to be good enough that I didn't give Barbara an opportunity to give to me and to feel close to me. My lesson took the form of a knee injury I suffered while playing basketball at 39 years old.

I had been playing basketball regularly with my daughters when they were 13 and 14 years old. Then, over the course of a few days my left knee began to swell. Months went by, and the swelling would not go down. I could bend the knee only a tiny bit. Pain became a constant part of my life. Walking was a slow, painful process; I resigned myself to arthroscopic knee surgery.

Although this occurred when I was 39, I remember it as though it were yesterday. Being a patient was disorienting. I had not been in a hospital as a patient since I was 13, when I had a liver biopsy. Now I was on the receiving end of medical care at my own hospital. The staff was very caring and professional. Barbara was very attentive to my every whim. Her touch was loving and gentle as the attendants wheeled me into the operating room.

They transferred me to the operating table and began the usual procedure of pre-surgical scrubbing on my left leg, but it was *my* leg! The anesthesiologists pricked and poked my back for the spinal anesthesia that would numb my body from the waist down. That didn't work entirely according to plan, as I could still feel my knee, although not as keenly as I would have otherwise. The spinal was at my request; I wanted to remain conscious during the surgery and listen to inspirational tapes.

I started the tape and let myself go into a world of celestial music and unlimited possibilities. I felt every cut and poke and twist of my knee, but that pain was just part of a magnificent process of healing. Having so many people giving to me all at once was amazing. I breathed deeply, transforming the pain into gratitude for the joyous possibility of playing basketball once again with my daughters. Even as the galaxies in the sky move through an exchange of giving and receiving with each other, I was moved to tears to feel my own participation in the celestial dance. I experienced myself as part of the dance of giving and receiving. There I was on the receiving end, and I was so grateful for the love and intelligent care that these wonderfully skilled people were bestowing on me.

In the past, I had dismissed others' appreciation of me as a physician and dedicated healer, a caring father, and lover to my wife. I had been a committed giver, but would not emotionally receive other's appreciation of me. Paradoxically, I was intensely seeking approval from others as a giver, even as I resisted accepting love as a receiver. The aspect of feeling controlled by others' approval had frightened me, but now, on that operating room table I was swept up by gratitude for the healers who were repairing my knee.

There is no movement without give and take. In order to give, someone must receive. Giving and receiving are part of the same process. I was now taking in all the love and years of dedication to excellence the medical staff was giving me. I felt blessed. I began crying with joy. Surprised, the anesthesiologist asked, "Are you all right?"

"Yes," I said. "I am just so happy."

Soon the operation was over. I cried more as I thanked each one present for their years of study and dedication to make my enjoyment of playing sports with my children possible once again. Although I had been a physician for more than 15 years, I had never realized how much a person could appreciate what a doctor does.

The next few days were an extraordinary experience of Barbara's nurturing care. I allowed her to dress and undress me, to wait on my every wish for food and ice packs, to help me to the bathroom. It was odd, but she said she felt closer to me by my willingness to receive her attention than she ever did before. It seemed like a game to let her give to me, but that was what was moving the stars, and who was I to argue with that? Even today, when I allow people to give to me I still experience the majesty of the celestial dance.

However, I still had more lessons to learn about letting love into my heart.

# Chapter 4

# Giving Up Complaints

You would think that the metaphors of the whirlpool in the computer game and the fence around the tree would have exhausted their value to me, but actually, they continued to be meaningful to my growth and transformation. While Barbara was a Ph.D. student, she encouraged me to attend some personal growth classes with her; the classes focused on looking at one's complaints about life, such as:

The reason I am unhappy is….

The reason I am not more successful is….

The reason why my life is not working is….

Barbara was always encouraging me to take courses on emotional and psychological growth in the traditions of Western culture. Left on my own, I would just meditate, which allows me to simply withdraw from her and worldly concerns. But she has a different way of growing, and it challenges my way of thinking about who I am. So despite my initial resistance, I took the course and found many tools that the course taught to be unexpectedly helpful.

In one class, I realized that my life complaint was a belief that my mother thought that I was not good enough, that she neither appreciated nor loved me in the ways I wanted. That belief created an expectation that other people in my life, such as Barbara, would or at least should make up for that deficit. When I didn't get the satisfaction I wanted, another complaint erupted. I was a complaint looking for an excuse to happen, and I was not experiencing even the love that was already present in my life.

In fact, my whole life until then was an attempt to show the world how good I was, so that everyone would appreciate me and eventually word would get back to my mother that I really was a great person. That was my motivation to be the best doctor. That was my motivation to have everyone like me. The irony was, I was so busy working as a doctor to prove that I was good enough, that I was not behaving with a loving heart in my marriage!

That realization caused me to see that my grudges and resentments concerning my mother were getting in the way of my desire for Barbara's love and appreciation. It became clear to me that I had to give up these resentments. I was no different from anyone else. I carried a big complaint around like a burden, and that explained the heaviness in my life.

## *Learning to Accept Our Parents*

An early memory, from when I was about eight years old, epitomizes my feeling of not being good enough. My parents came home from working in the family store as usual at 8:00 p.m. My mother expected the house to be neat and clean. After working all day, she did not want more cleaning to do when she got home. That evening, after I finished a glass of water, I left the glass in the sink, thinking that I would use it again before long. In my mind, I was trying to keep the house as neat as possible. But when my mother came home, she started yelling as mothers do when they are not happy. "How could you not wash out a single glass and put it upside down in the dish drainer?" I remember that she yelled for almost an hour about how ungrateful I was. My ears were hurting because she yelled so loudly. This memory lived and grew in my mind as a story to prove how I wasn't appreciated, and how I was unfairly criticized.

I created an interpretation that my mother did not appreciate me, that I was not good enough. And as the case is for all of us, I formed this significant interpretation when I was a very young child. Such interpretations have colored my perspective ever since. I incorporated that story into my identity. It persisted until much later in life explaining my continuing sensitivities. I kept bumping into that feeling of being unappreciated and criticized, and of course that only created more problems for me. The story became my excuse for my poor performance as a husband.

Giving up the hope that my mother would finally love me in a way that made me feel good enough was very difficult. I had struggled my entire life to feel loved and appreciated by her. Just considering the process placed a heavy weight on my heart; I had to give up the hope that my mother would ever love me the way that I wanted her to love me. I just would love my mom for who she was and for the limited kindness she was capable of showing.

This turned out to be another paradoxical process. As I accepted that I created the belief that I was not good enough, I was able to accept my mother as she was. Letting go of the expectation that my mother would be truly comforting to me reminded me of the metaphor of the maple tree. The tree accepted the fence as it was, and did not reject or resist it. The tree transcended the fence by making it a part of itself. I too had to accept the way that my feeling not good enough had been limiting me. I had to accept my mother with her limitations of not being effusively loving and nurturing. Yet with that acceptance, I gained the hope of transcending the limitations of that fence and my needy personality.

I started to call my mother every week on the phone, as that always made her very happy. She only required five-minute phone calls, and to tell the truth, in the past it had annoyed me to place them. But after letting go of that life complaint, I called her every week and it began to change our relationship. I begin to do more things that made her happy, like sending cards and flowers. In the past, I had always begrudged doing those things. But to my surprise, the cards and flowers seemed to cheer her up immensely. Over time, she began to think of me as her wonderful son, and that change seemed to cheer up Barbara. So, giving up those grudges toward my mother allowed me to better fulfill the requests that Barbara was making of me.

It was like learning a new language of love—a sea change in my worldview. These new behaviors and attitudes began to change my relationship with Barbara. I stopped resisting the small efforts that she seemed to appreciate so well. I gave her a hug when I left in the morning and when I came home at night. I held the car door open for her on a date night. I saved her a seat when we went to a meeting or a class. I created personal time for us on a weekly basis. I sent her endearing notes in sweet cards. The results of doing so were transformative. I had no idea that doing those little things for the women in my life would make them so happy.

Letting go of lifelong complaints did not happen overnight. It was a gradual process of accepting the reality of my childhood, accepting my mother as she was, and releasing my disappointments. Pleasing Barbara and feeling her appreciation helped me immensely in the process. A big part of the journey toward maturity is coming to terms with your parents—particularly the parent with whom you had the most difficulty. My mother was very demanding. My dad was easygoing.

My relationship with my mother continued to evolve over the years. She felt I had become extremely caring and attentive, and we developed a very sweet relationship. The change, however, did not translate to others in my family. They continued to resist her demanding nature, and she continued to be very demanding to them. Paradoxically, I transformed my difficult relationships with my mother and Barbara through accepting them as they were, neither reacting to them nor expecting them to change. I believe that is a principle that will work for anyone who wants to transform a difficult relationship into a caring and loving one.

Some years after our first personal growth class designed to give up your complaints about life, and after many years of conducting attitudinal healing classes, Barbara suggested we take that first class over again. But reviewing that old learning didn't make sense to me. Nevertheless, Barbara wanted to do it, and I agreed to go with her. When the idea of the life-complaint came up again, I had nothing to argue about. I had no questions. I had no objections. I completely agreed with everything they had to say about it, unlike the first time around, when I had resisted the idea that I was making up a life-complaint from my own interpretations of life events.

My response to rehearing all that information was that during the breaks I would go into the bathroom and cry. I would come out for more of the class, and during the next break I would go to the bathroom and cry again. What in heaven's name was going on? What was I grieving about or for?

When I think about that day now, it was like a death in the family. Seven years prior, I had intellectually accepted the idea that I needed to give up my complaint about my mother. This time around, I emotionally and fully let go of my resistance to loving her and letting love into my life. The crying was an emotional release from all those years of feeling hurt. Letting go of one's life complaint is pivotal to opening one's heart to truly loving significant people in your life, such as your wife or mother. One's ego stubbornly holds on to those continuing complaints. Letting go is a very intense emotional process.

It was like surrendering to a whirlpool. I was open to letting go, and willing to search and wander in the watery world of emotions. I let go of my complaint that my mother did not think I was good enough, by accepting what was, as the tree took the metal fence into itself. I accepted that my complaint was just an interpretation that had no intrinsic reality. I moved beyond that limited interpretation and expanded into a new realm.

# Chapter 5

# Percival and the Grail:
# The Masculine Spiritual Quest

## *Moving from Warrior towards Wise Elder*

I could hardly believe it. My father was dying. He was healthy and vigorous for his 72 years—rarely sick until he contracted pneumonia six months before his fatal diagnosis. While he was sick, I flew from LA to New York almost every other week to be with him. We were very close when I was young. I remember his patience in teaching me and my two brothers how to drive a car, run the dry-cleaning machine for our family business, and fix a flat tire or a broken electrical plug. His education took him only through eighth grade, and he was very careful never to put anyone down for slow learning. He made me feel so appreciated, so empowered to be great. He wanted his three boys to do better than he did.

During the 12 years I was living in California, however, I grew distant from him. He was a practical man who dealt with life in the moment. He was not a letter writer, and he did not talk much on the phone. Finally, he was in denial about his impending death, even as he steadily lost strength week by week. The cancer was spreading despite all the chemotherapy and radiation treatments.

Barbara coached me to make my time with my father more meaningful on those visits, but I was frightened to talk to him from my heart. She encouraged me to avoid complaining to the medical staff and trying medical techniques to help him. "What else is there?" I asked. "Dad doesn't want to talk about dying. He changes the subject. He gets angry. He says he needs to rest. My mother has not left his bedside in three weeks. She terrorizes the hospital staff. My brothers wouldn't stand for it if I said anything that upset Dad."

Barbara answered, "Just tell your dad how much he means to you. Tell him why your life is so blessed by what he gave to you."

That, of course, was the scariest thing I could think of doing. I felt a lump in my throat whenever I thought of talking like that to my father. He was a man of jokes, action, and of direct expression, not of feelings-talk and psychological reflection.

## *Intimate Conversation with My Father*

Finally, the moment came. I reached the hospital room. My mother was angry with the nurses. My father was depressed and withdrawn. He was barely talking to anyone. My brother told me, "It's been like this for almost two weeks." My heart was racing; my hands were trembling. I walked over to my dad, who was lying in bed, and sat down next to him. "Hi, Dad," I said. He opened his eyes and nodded. He seemed weak and fatigued.

"Dad, I've been thinking about things and wanted you to know how much you mean to me in my life."

"Michael," he interrupted sharply. "What do you want from me?"

"Dad, I just want you to listen to me. You don't need to say anything." My dad seemed to quiet down, so I continued.

"Dad, you gave me the confidence that I could do anything. Your endless patience taught me how to repair all kinds of things. You made me feel capable. You never put me down or yelled at me for how I did something. You just taught me with love. I remember learning to drive on your knee, to steer the big steering wheel of our green 1956 Plymouth, with your guiding hand to help me." My dad opened his eyes wide and looked right at me.

I continued, "You taught me how to look at something broken and think, 'How does this work?' Then take it apart until I saw how it was supposed to work. I learned from you to look at all the breakdowns in life like that—mechanical things, business things, and relationships." By now, my racing heart had quieted down. My dad continued to look intently at me as I went on talking to him softly.

"You taught me how to do everything about running the family dry-cleaning business. I felt I could learn anything. You gave me the gift of loving life's challenges and enjoying the process of solving life's problems. Dad, I love who you are to me. I am so fulfilled that you are my father. Thank you."

My father reached out for my hand. His hands were bigger, thicker, and heavier than anyone's hands I've ever known. But his touch was the warmest and most loving touch imaginable, as his hand gently covered mine. My eyes filled with tears of joy. My father's eyes similarly filled with tears, and his mouth moved slightly into a peaceful smile. It was a moment that lives in my heart as an eternal living presence of love.

"Dad, I know that you don't believe there is anything after this life. But I feel certain you are going on another journey. You always kidded that the man upstairs looked out for you. You said he would hold off the rain for our dry-cleaning business until we closed. When your car got a flat tire in a remote area in Italy during your vacation with Mom and there was no jack to change the flat, you prayed for help. Then, within two minutes God sent you a priest with the exact jack you needed. Dad, I know that God will not desert you now. He will take care of you in this life and the next."

After an eternity of love-filled moments, my father sprung to life. He sat up and said, "Why is everyone outside the room? Call them in!" For the last two weeks of his life, he was animated and joyful with everyone. He gathered the immediate family around him and dictated goodbyes to everyone in his life in his simple loving way.

Like Percival, I found my Holy Grail through the risk of being emotionally present and feeling deep connections with the important individuals in my life.

## *The Story of Percival*

The story of Percival, or Parsifal or Parzival, one of King Arthur's knights, encapsulates the masculine spiritual quest. It begins with Percival, as an innocent teenager, becoming enflamed with a passion to become a knight. Percival's mother had raised him in the forest away from all knightly things. She detested knighthood because his father was a renowned  knight who was killed in a fight when Percival was just an infant. His mother only told him about angels and love.

Percival is possessed of tremendous natural skills and learns on his own how to throw a wooden spear at birds. As he kills them, he cries when they die, but he loves the game. One day when Percival is a teenager, a band of knights on horses passes by. Percival bows down and says, "Are you angels?"

"No. We are knights. Do not bow down to us," they answered.

"How do I become a knight?" questions Percival.

"Go down the road to King Arthur's court." And the knights ride off.

Percival's soul is called by this quest to be a knight. Like his father, Percival has tremendous natural skills but is completely untrained. Then, through a long series of episodes, he receives training in knighthood etiquette and swordsmanship, and becomes a knight. All men possess natural skills and abilities which must be groomed and focused by social conventions for worldly success.

Sometime later, Percival marries for love, refusing to marry for position or wealth. Other than marrying for love, Percival follows to the best of his ability all social expectations of knighthood. He becomes the most esteemed of knights, extremely successful, and loved and admired by all. He reaches the pinnacle of masculine achievement. Then, he receives an invitation to the Fisher King's mystical Grail Castle, which was under a magical curse. The Fisher King suffers from a grave wound and is in terrible pain. But as caretaker of the Grail, he cannot die, only live in suffering.

The spell over the castle affects everything and everyone within its walls. All hope for the arrival of a pure knight who can heal the Fisher King and break the spell by asking a question from his heart, "Oh King, what ails thee?" However, the spell prevents anyone from helping Percival ask the heartfelt question.

When Percival arrives, he witnesses a strange ceremony, but suppresses the natural inclination of his heart and instead behaves as his social education as a knight had taught him: A knight does not ask questions unless he is asked first. Therefore, Percival fails to ask the ailing Fisher King the question that would have broken the spell.

Percival later learns, to his devastation, that had he asked the obvious question he was feeling at the castle, the Fisher King would have been healed, the curse over the castle broken, and he would have achieved the Holy Grail. Like most men, Percival suppressed his own heartfelt concern and instead acted according to the social convention of the day.

Nevertheless, after he leaves the Grail castle, he receives grand acclaim as the greatest knight in the land, and King Arthur invites him to sit at the Round Table. But when the news gets out about his failing to heal the Fisher King and behold the Holy Grail, he suffers public humiliation and dishonor.

To win back his honor, Percival then spends many years attempting to return to the Grail castle and achieve his quest. He persists even though everyone tells him that what he is attempting is impossible. He despairs, thinking that, although he did everything that he was taught to do as a good knight, God still deserted him. He becomes angry and resentful of his situation. Yet he continues searching for the Grail castle, with one adventure following the other.

One important milestone was coming to the hermitage of a retired knight, who relates Percival's entire painful, family history to him. Percival then realizes the spiritual vision of his life, gains compassion for those he has injured, and atones for his shortcomings. He accepts that his failings are part of God's greater plan for him, and learns true love and grace.

Percival then continues on his quest, and enters into battle against a foreign knight. His sword breaks, and it seems as though the foreign knight is about to win. Yet the other knight refuses to kill an unarmed foe, and reveals himself to be Percival's half-brother. This episode teaches Percival the lesson of humility and accepting defeat. His trials and inner growth continue through even more adventures, until at last Percival miraculously is allowed to return to the Grail Castle. There he asks the question from his heart, heals the Fisher King, and attains the Holy Grail. He regains the company of his wife and becomes the new Grail King.

## Personalizing Percival

The inability to speak authentically and act from one's heart, acting rather out of learned, social conventions, can be a wound in the psyche of men and some career women who have adopted a male ethos. Men need to recognize their emotional connections with others and speak from their heart in order to become whole individuals. Women face the same developmental challenge, but typically learn emotional intimacy in a time sequence different from the one that most men follow. Although Percival's story is a masculine story, ultimately both genders need to learn how to be intimate.

Men appreciate the value of intimacy later in life than women. Women identify with connection earlier than men, especially if they are raising children. A man's world of business and career requires independent thinking and a strong ego. Women who establish a career before marrying often experience life through the masculine growth model, as their careers may demand that they put off the qualities of intimacy and nurturing. Expressing one's feelings is usually inappropriate in the business world. After a man (or a career woman) achieves success, they then need to learn to feel and share deep emotional connections if they wish to continue their personal development. Learning the lessons of humility and intimacy are necessary, as success-oriented individuals in business, sports, or other competitive careers will use success to keep intimacy at a distance. The irony is that society often acclaims successful career persons, even when they are not so successful at home in their personal lives.

A strong sense of self, a strong ego, is essential for success in the world of achievements. But through countless examples, we know that the world of achievements never produces a whole person. To attain what Western culture calls "the Holy Grail," an individual must connect to the realm of the soul. To experience God's presence (in secular terms, a sense of wholeness), every man must complete the masculine journey. For some, it is developing a deeper love for others. For others, it may be fulfilling a passion to creating something of great benefit to others. Although the myths and stories of the Grail vary, it is usually depicted as a chalice cup or a stone. It always, however, symbolizes God's presence here on earth.

Many young men (and some young women) get a glimpse of the realm of the soul that stimulates them to pursue their quest, a passionate call to do something big in this life. Some individuals have a quest for business and achieving wealth. Others quest for achieving fame. Some quest for success in sports.

I had a quest to discover the meaning of life, which I first realized during my illness when I was 13 years old. I needed to resolve my anxiety, fear, and horror of death. (When I was 16, I read Hermann Hesse's *Siddhartha*, which ignited a passion in me to achieve the Buddhist conception of enlightenment.)

Like Percival, I had many adventures, which I have shared, in my quest to obtain my Holy Grail. Being sent home from Switzerland by my meditation teacher was to me failing to reach the Holy Grail in my first attempt. Then, when my father became ill with inoperable lung cancer, that became my second chance to reach the Holy Grail. Sharing my gratitude with my father was the scariest and most intimate conversation I've ever had.

In the Grail story, Percival's heartfelt and intimate conversation with the Fisher King heals the king's wound and restores him and his kingdom to vitality. It was the healing for which the king had been waiting. In Percival's first attempt, he was unable to break through the social conventions of politeness. It is that breakthrough in intimacy that is so critical for the king and the kingdom's health, as it was for my father and for my emotional well-being.

Ten days after I returned to California, I heard that my father had been passing into and out of a coma due to kidney failure. I also learned to my surprise, that, while he was conscious he positively shocked the hospital staff, doctors, nurses, and his aides with his loving enthusiasm. So, I went back to New York, hoping to be with my father when he passed on and to be a comfort to him and ease his fear of dying. On my way to the hospital, I had a thought to pick up a Jewish prayer book for him.

In some versions of the Percival story, after the Fisher King's realm revives, he retires and transfers the care of the Grail to Percival, who then becomes the Grail King. I thought I was giving comfort to my father in his passing, but in fact the gift I received was far greater than whatever I gave.

As Dad went in and out of consciousness, I read the prayer book out loud to him in Hebrew and English for many hours. I stopped only to talk with my mother about our beliefs in life and death. She had many doubts. I shared my certainty, as many of my patients had experiences of dying and returning to the body.

When my father finally stopped breathing, I was surprised at the depth of my grief. I thought my belief in life after death would make it an easy transition for me, but instead I fell into an overwhelming heaviness. I could not see anything but my father's body lying on the bed. I felt totally lost. I opened the prayer book to the next page.

"The Lord is my shepherd I shall not want... Though I walk through the valley of the shadow of death I shall fear no evil... My cup runneth over... Goodness and mercy will follow me all the days of my life."

I felt someone reaching out to me who understood how I was feeling, as generations of my ancestors have felt as they stood at their fathers' deathbeds. I felt simultaneously the great loss of my father and the profound support of the generations of spiritual fathers of my tradition. I thought I was giving a gift to my father by reading prayers to make his passing more comfortable. But in reality, my father gave me the gift of allowing prayers to personally support me and open my heart. I was falling into the whirlpool again, but now I had support and new trust.

For several years after my father's passing, whenever I thought of him I would cry. It would happen many times a day, not from sadness, but rather from a love so sublime that it brought tears to my eyes. My father's gift to me was the intense experience of opening my heart and the feeling of divine love entering in.

My father's passing changed the way I experienced God. Before that, God was an impersonal force that gave me a feeling of peace and joy. But afterwards, God became a personally intense experience of being loved with a purity and limitlessness that moved into all parts of my being. To move from an abstract belief in God to a personal relationship with God is an important breakthrough for any man or woman. Feeling deeply loved by someone like your father creates an opportunity for God to enlarge that love into an experience of unbounded love. That, at least, was my experience.

It changed the way I love people. After being filled with so much love, I could in turn love my wife, and love her intensely in a more deeply personal way. It allowed me to love my wife as she needed to be loved. I did what she found to be loving, whether or not it made sense to me. That is the nature of successful personal relationships. You do the things that your partner finds loving because you care about her feelings and her perceptions.

## Getting Beyond the Ego

My male mentality had a hard time accepting the value of being vulnerable. I believed that appearing successful and competent was the highest form of personal development. That limited perspective about showing vulnerability was evident to me when Barbara and I would watch a minister on TV who shared her life struggles and problems with her viewers. To my astonishment, the minister would cry and reveal her personal conflicts in front of her television audience. She would use her private issues to illustrate spiritual principles. It shocked my sensibilities that a person would demonstrate his or her "high level" of individual growth by sobbing on television. Other ministers I saw crying on television befuddled me. How could this be an indication of spiritual leadership?

It took me a long time to understand this. Barbara and I spent 12 years studying and leading classes in attitudinal healing as taught by Jerry Jampolsky. Those classes taught me how to be open to the world of feelings and to simultaneously think clearly and apply spiritual principles.

The journey of adult life can have many stages. For men and many career women, early adulthood is a time to focus on building a stable sense of self that is competent, capable, and successful in the world. Later adulthood may move the ego into a transparent, secondary role that allows a more authentic self to find expression. As you grow in acceptance, love, and confidence, you have opportunities to heal deeper layers of old hurts and resentments. That allows a bigger vision of life and greater appreciation and deeper love for others. When your ego becomes more transparent, looking good fades in importance.

I believe that every man can find his Holy Grail through risking emotional openness and feeling deep connections with those whom he loves. In our marriage classes, I've seen men grow their skills for intimacy. The process is a journey that takes time and requires a sometimes-difficult inner transformation to dissolve the blockages to love. Opening my heart to loving others is a gift that continues to unfold in my life. Healing old wounds seems to be an ever-deepening process that gradually gives birth to a love that is intense and unbounded.

# Chapter 6

# Saving My Mother's Life, and Her Gift to Me

### Living the Wise Elder Stage

When my mother was 76, she suffered life-threatening complications from back surgery. Her hometown doctors were just going to let her die. But my brothers and I decided to fly her to my hospital in California. I directed a team of doctors who worked on her for about a month. After she regained consciousness, she continued to recover, and she lived for another six years.

She thanked me deeply for saving her life, and enjoyed bragging to anyone who would listen about how I saved her life. It was a dream come true for an eight-year-old boy who hungered for his mother's appreciation.

Two weeks before she died, she had a stroke. She was living in Florida then, and I flew from California to see her the day I got the news. She could speak only one- or two-word sentences. When she saw me, her eyes opened wide, she smiled, and held my hands. Her face was beaming with love as she said, "Michael," in a sweet voice, and then repeated my name in that loving voice for three minutes because she couldn't say anything else. Her loving voice, her soft touch, and shining face repeating my name remains a cherished gift that fills my being to this very day.

Not all stories have such a happy ending. Yet I believe that when you give up your personal life complaints, you gain opportunities for complete healing. For me, allowing myself to show my mother my love for her, and letting go of my life complaint of not being appreciated, gave me a much greater intimacy with both her and Barbara and with everyone else in my life as well.

Successful men are often full of themselves in the first parts of their lives. In the second part of a successful man's life, it may be necessary to hear the voices of wisdom, love, and compassion. The process for me was letting go of things I thought were critical for my ego. That seems to be how God works in my life. He takes something away from me that I thought I wanted only to give me something much more precious. I had to let go of the resentment around my feelings of not having my mother's appreciation. When I completely gave up wishing for what I never would have, I received the much more precious gift of unbounded love.

I gave up my self-righteous anger and gained an ability to listen to and appreciate others' points of view. I gave up feeling superior to others in the community, and I gained the experience of intimacy with them and many others. When I gave up the idea that just one more meditation retreat would enable me to reach my goal of spiritual enlightenment, I gained a deeper intimacy in my marriage, and the gift of personal love from Barbara was greater than my intellectual idea of spiritual growth.

I gave up being a medical doctor to my dying father, and I gained an opening in my heart to deeply and personally love others. When he passed away, I lost him physically, but gained an intimate presence of his love. When my mother passed on, I lost her physically, but gained a deeper connection to her love and appreciation of my accomplishments.

A man's realization of the Holy Grail slowly unfolds in the second half of life. It requires him to transform from a warrior conquering the world to a wise elder who lets go of a limited perspective to embrace intimate relationships with others in his life.

# Part 3

## Barbara's Story

# Chapter 7

# The Journey of Marriage:
# Moving into Caretaker Stage

I was a very young woman when I first fell in love with Michael. We had a natural affinity for philosophy and spirituality, and our conversations were very enjoyable. He was a moral person, and I felt he would be loyal and honorable. Those were important values for me, though I would not have been able to articulate that at the time. We also had a very sweet and natural chemistry. Against my parents' advice, we married two weeks shy of my twenty-first birthday.

Soon, Michael started his intensive hospital rotation as a third-year medical student. I started graduate school and filled myself with new learning. Michael enjoyed discussing my academic work. Much of the time, he would be at the hospital or sleeping as I did my school work. When he had time off, he would go to meditation courses, which meant a lot to him. Most times I would join him, but if that didn't work with my schedule, he would go by himself.

When Michael told me how important it was for him to become a meditation teacher, I decided to support him and arranged my schedule to be in Switzerland for three months. At that time, it was just my way to accommodate. I justified the adventure as an opportunity to learn at the feet of a meditation master. After all, I was a theology student, and meditation had some relevance to my interests. Years followed when I meditated, intermittently taught meditation, and completed a master's degree. There are few feelings assigned to these events because I did not know my feelings in those days. When I look back now, I see that I enjoyed learning with Michael and meeting people, but the meditation community was not an intimate environment. It reinforced my lack of emotional development. The hours of solitary meditation reminded me of my lonely childhood, and I did not know how to say that I was a lonely adult.

When my grandmother died, the pain of losing her ignited my desire to have a family. I was twenty-four, and at a crossroads in my career with no immediate plans. It seemed like a good time to have a baby and fill my heart with new love. Michael planned to work as a medical doctor for a meditation community in Switzerland, and I, already pregnant, would have the baby there. When we arrived, the community persuaded us to participate in a meditation course. Michael had not planned on this, but the spiritual carrots that the retreat promised left him unable to say no. And I was still accommodating.

## Breaking the Rules and Seeing the Face of Relationships in the Light - *Transition from Caretaker to Warrior*

After several more extended, residential meditation courses it began to dawn on me that I could not do this anymore. The final straw was a two-month course in Switzerland. We packed up our two-year-old and five-month-old daughters with their nannies, but we could not keep the children on campus. Michael succeeded in finding an apartment for them within walking distance, and we saw them at lunch and dinner. Toward the end of the course, I found a room on campus with a private entrance and broke the rules so the babies could stay with me at night. I was sad to be apart from my babies, but I was a cooperative wife.

I don't think I realized until then how unhappy I was, because the children filled my heart, and Michael and I had been collaborating a lot together. I had managed a meditation center at our home in Eureka so he could teach. Our conversations were always interesting and intellectual.

When we returned to California, I knew I had to make a change. I had to go back to school and finish my education. I heard my New York professor had moved to Southern California. I told Michael it was time I went back to school. He had completed his contract with the hospital, so we moved to Southern California, and Michael started a private practice.

## *Feeling Bereft*

When Michael started his private practice, we stepped into a whole new world of complexity. He had not only to practice medicine, but he also needed to run a business, and for that he needed a lot of support in consultants and staff. His workday was extremely long, and the office manager, whoever it was, was his right arm.

Early on there was a woman, I will call her Sally, who worked for Michael and who was interested in more than just the job. She would flirt, even when I was present. One day, I overheard her husband call on the phone; he was having a panic attack and needed reassurance about her love. That was when I knew I wasn't misconstruing her behaviors. Over the years there were several employees who were flirtatious and manipulative. But that was my first experience of that kind of disrespectful intrusion into my marriage.

I may have been willing to accept Michael's lack of emotional authenticity for as long as I did because I thought those were his limitations. But one day he came to me and said that he felt closer to Sally than me; I was threatened to my core. I hardly noticed the emotional intelligence and integrity it took for him to confide in me with that information. He was really inviting me to be closer to him, but my pain and fear distracted me too much to realize it.

My pain astonished me. If I had been another woman with a different history, perhaps I would have felt less pain, or handled it more effectively. But I was overwhelmed with fears of loss. Those fears hearkened back to when I was two. That was when my parents divorced, and my mother believed it was best to end all contact with my biological father. I hardly knew him. Years later when she remarried, I again grieved the loss that only children have with their single mothers. I also felt she monopolized my stepfather, especially when she was suffering a lengthy illness.

So when Michael told me about his feelings for Sally, I began reliving my childhood wounds. Pain and anger paralyzed me. I became critical, attacking, hurt, and confused. If I had been intellectual before, I was in the chaotic world of feelings now. I was behaving miserably to Michael, and I had no skills to calm myself or express myself rationally.

I came to realize years later that Michael's closeness to his staff and his yearning for my partnership in his office came from the model his parents had set. They worked together in the family dry-cleaning business. His mother would go to the store every day at 2:00 p.m. and close the store with his father at 7:00 p.m. Then they would drive home together, often having dinner at a restaurant on the way. Michael and his brothers would eat dinner, often cooked by a housekeeper, and their parents expected them to clean up after themselves.

Michael likewise knew my parents' routine: My father would come home from Wall Street by subway to Queens. My mother would have a gourmet dinner on the table at 6:00 p.m. Oddly, I followed my mother's pattern rather than adapt to Michael's. I continued for years making early dinner, expecting Michael to come home and eat with the family, while he expected me to be his partner in the office. Both of us held unexpressed and unfulfilled desires.

Neither of us articulated our unconscious expectations of fulfilling our parents' models until things exploded in the issue of Sally, probably because that touched my abandonment wounds. The upset opened up all the other disappointments and hurts that had been accumulating over the years of our unconscious marriage. Michael's connection to someone on his staff hurt me deeply, especially after all the years of emotional absence and devotion to a meditation organization.

At the time, his model of a better relationship was working shoulder to shoulder in the office like his parents. That vision may have been possible if I were an office manager kind of person. At his request, I did a stint of working at his office, but it was not a fit. I knew I needed to follow my own path. It had worked for us when I managed the meditation center, but I was now defining myself and I had my own destiny to fulfill.

It turned out that I was no more emotionally developed than Michael. My fear and anger about Sally brought me to the realization that I had to work on myself and rebuild our marriage. Sally was not the problem; the quality of our marriage was. I needed to work on my childhood hurts that had created those irrational fears.

Michael also had childhood wounds that needed to be resolved. My response to his feelings was reminiscent of his mother's criticism. Both of us were touching old pain even as we were reaching for new love and respect. It was a challenge to create a new and positive dynamic that was more intimate and fulfilling, and it initiated our conscious journey to create love. That quest included an individual and a relationship project for each of us.

Ultimately, I stopped Sally's mischievous behavior myself. One day, I arranged to speak with her privately, acknowledged her attractiveness, and asked her to stop flirting with my husband. I remember her smiling. She liked the compliment and did not seem embarrassed by my confrontation. Nevertheless, her behavior stopped, and eventually she left. I had been waiting for Michael to find a solution for me, only to discover that I could do it myself. Had I known sooner, I could have saved us many upsets.

## Growing Autonomy

I knew I needed to grow. I could not help Michael in the office. I had to find my independence and learn to be okay when Michael was unhappy with me. He was often unhappy with me, and in those days, it would crush me. He would make decisions unilaterally and they would always sound so noble that I had a hard time making a case for my point of view.

Once, Michael told me that I was an obstacle to his spiritual growth! I was shocked and felt that the problem was spiritual growth as he conceived it. To help me make my case, I became an expert in ego and faith development.

I went back to school. I did a pastoral counseling internship at St. Joseph Hospital in Orange, California. My supervisor was a man named George Markham who had been a Baptist minister. He became my mentor. My life started changing because I was learning to connect my feelings and thoughts. I also began to internalize the respect I was receiving from George and my peers. This gave me the confidence to develop myself.

An important moment occurred one night when I invited George to have dinner with me and my two children. Michael called from his meditation retreat in Los Angeles. He was thinking of extending for an extra week and wanted to know what I thought about it. I was enjoying my evening, and I found myself saying to Michael, "Do whatever you want." To my utter surprise, Michael was home the next morning with a beautiful cosmetic mirror for me, a gift that I treasure to this day.

I learned a lot from that moment. I stopped running after Michael and felt more centered. I began to understand more deeply the words of the famous family counselor, Carl Whitaker: "A self is more attractive than a non-self." My new independence was an early important step that put us on the road together. We still did not know much about how to create the marriage, but I had Michael's attention.

Slowly, with focused intention, I earned my self-respect as well as Michael's respect by gaining competence in my work and in my thinking process. Over time, I was able to rationally present my point of view about how good relationships contribute to mature spirituality in a way that meditation by itself cannot. This has been a dynamic conversation over decades that has been rewarding for both of us. At the same time, I found resources for us to grow emotionally and express our deeper feelings and thoughts. This has grown our marriage. Michael consistently responded with a willingness to match my energy for developing himself as well as our lives together. Step by step we learned to stretch ourselves and teach each other what we want and need from each other.

It took years to create a partnership I felt graced to be in. This has led us to understand the dynamics of adult development and how marriage can provide a creative friction that stimulates greater self-understanding as well as a bridge to an authentic and satisfying partnership.

# Chapter 8

# The Story of the Greek Goddess Psyche

I see myself in the story of Psyche and Eros. The character of Psyche represents an archetypal female personality. Her story illustrates how Western civilization understands the dynamics of love and individuality. I believe that Psyche offers us a blueprint of how a woman comes to a relationship and then differentiates. Psyche offers us a view to the struggle that ensues, and the ultimate partnership that can blossom out of her personal development.

Psyche is the only Greek goddess who gave up her divinity because she was so in love with the possibilities of life in the physical world. She was born to a king and queen, and was extraordinarily beautiful. No man would marry her because all could only worship her in her beauty. No one could love her as an individual. Psyche's beauty was so overwhelming that when the god of passion, Eros (the Cupid of Roman mythology), saw her, he accidentally pricked himself with one of his own arrows, and so fell madly in love with her and married her.

Eros made Psyche promise him that she would never look at his face and she would only be with him in the dark of night. That restriction aside, Psyche and Eros had a beautiful marriage. They made love every night in his magnificent castle in the mountains. Soon, Psyche became pregnant, and lonely. To ease her lonely daytime hours, Psyche invited her sisters to visit her. They were jealous of her happiness and the beauty and wealth of her surroundings, so they sowed doubt into Psyche's mind, taunting her with the suggestion that her husband was really a demon monster who would eventually kill her and their child.

As her doubts increased, Psyche rose one night when Eros was sleeping and lit a candle to see if, in fact, her loving husband was a monster demon. When the candle shone on him, she saw the most beautiful, handsome, radiant face she could imagine. She was so amazed that her hand trembled, and some hot wax spilled from the candle onto Eros, waking him. Eros turned to Psyche and said, "You have broken your promise. I am leaving you now."

Psyche fell into a deep despair, and like Percival, went on a long journey. However, unlike Percival, her journey was motivated by her desire to reclaim her relationship with Eros. This journey required developing skills and finding inner strengths. She sought help from Eros's mother, Aphrodite, the goddess of beauty. But Aphrodite was jealous of Psyche's beauty and cruelly agreed to reunite Psyche with Eros only if Psyche could complete a series of seemingly impossible tasks.

## The Three Tasks

The first task involved separating seeds of individual types out of a huge pile of mixed seeds. Miraculously, Psyche was able to gain the help of an army of ants, and so achieved the task.

The second task involved collecting the golden wool from divine rams that were wild and violent. Psyche achieved this with supernatural coaching from reeds that grew by the riverside where the rams lived. The reeds told her to wait until dusk, when the dangerous rams settled down for the evening. Then she could pick up the golden strands of wool ensnared on the thorns of the briars growing there. She did so, and accomplished the seemingly impossible task.

Psyche's third task required her to collect water from the source of the magical River Styx in a crystal goblet. Mountainous crags, fierce dragons, and poisonous fumes surrounded the source, threatening any who might attempt to take water from this mystic spring. This time, she gained the aid of a divine eagle that took the goblet, swooped past the dragons and poisons, scooped up some of the Styx's water in the goblet, and brought it back to Psyche.

## Securing the Secret of Feminine Beauty

Frustrated by Psyche's miraculous ability to fulfill the first three tasks, Aphrodite at last commanded her to bring back from Persephone, queen of the underworld, an ointment that created beauty and youthfulness. Psyche despaired of fulfilling this task, and decided to kill herself by jumping from a tower. But the tower spoke to Psyche, instructing her to speak to no one in the underworld and to avoid helping any of the dead souls who would be begging for her help. "If you even lift a hand to help one of them you will never return," said the tower, who also told her to hold a loaf of barley bread in each hand and two gold coins in her mouth.

Psyche completed the final task with restraint and purpose. She ignored all the pitiful souls crying out for her help. She used the loaves of bread to distract Cerberus, the underworld's three-headed guard dog—giving him one on the way in and one on the way back. And she similarly used the two gold coins to pay Charon, the River Styx's ferryman, for her crossing into and out of the underworld.

On her way back to Mount Olympus, where Aphrodite lived, the pregnant Psyche was horrified by her bruised, bleeding, and disheveled appearance. So she decided to use some of the magical ointment that Aphrodite had demanded she bring back, because it would restore her beauty for her reunion with Eros. But upon opening the box that contained the ointment, Psyche died, as this special substance was only for the gods.

Safe passage to and from the underworld was the only task where supernatural help came from a manmade object, the tower, symbolizing the high level of individual human development necessary for that journey. It also symbolizes a conscious integration of all the earlier tasks. Quelling the fury of Cerberus with the loaves of bread represents Psyche's mastery of her physical and emotional needs. The gold coins she kept in her mouth represent her ability to control her speech. Further, she learned to discipline her desire to help and nurture others when they interfered with her highest purpose: to reunite with her husband and create their family. The ability to withhold kindness is sometimes a greater good than loving with unrestricted kindness. The myth of Psyche is a lesson about such boundaries. Learning to say "no" is a key to personal development.

## *Psyche's Transformation*

Eros was so moved by the person that Psyche had become through her ordeal that he left Mount Olympus and brought her back to life as an equal, symbolizing the transformation from Psyche's childlike nature to her development into a mature woman who was ready to partner with Eros. Women want and need to grow beyond the immaturity of Psyche's original relationship

with Eros, where he was totally in charge and she was living in the dark.

For all of Eros's "control," however, he was not fully developed himself. He had been the trickster who entertained himself by shooting his love arrows, and watching people struggle with the loves he forced upon them. Psyche was not Aphrodite's intended mate for her son, and Eros was not yet ready to stand up to his mother and claim his choice of a wife. Thus, Eros hid Psyche in the mountains and tried to avoid his dominating mother. Psyche's evolution as an individual moved Eros to step forward, declare his independence from his mother, and become Psyche's husband and true partner. The power of their love ultimately enabled both of them to grow.

In story form, this ancient myth outlines the developmental tasks that are the unique female quest to adult partnership with her husband: Psyche sorted out her dreams, conquered her instincts, and learned self-control. Then she learned to stop fighting against masculine energy. She found her personal identity, defined clear boundaries, and focused on her true priorities. The renowned psychiatrist, Carl Jung called this journey "individuation." Psyche claimed herself as an independent being and empowered herself to create the life she wanted. This could be any woman's story. This is my story.

# Chapter 9

# Seeing Love in the Light of Day

It is not hard to see myself in the story of Psyche and Eros. Eros asked her to love him without seeing him in the light—in other words, to be happy without emotional intimacy. I remember when those same terms were fine in my marriage, and I was genuinely happy. Then I needed to redefine the terms of our relationship because I had changed. I wanted a deeper emotional engagement with Michael. When I would attempt it, he would respond with anger and distance. I had shined the light on him and broken the unspoken rules of the relationship.

## *Taking Responsibility for Creating Love*

Michael's focus on meditation was hard for me because it had an idealistic value. It ennobled him. It was one of the reasons I loved him. His application of his passion, however, was selfish from my point of view, and it took me a decade to make my case. It would have been a lot easier if his hobby were basketball or cars. It would have been a lot harder if it were alcohol. But it was what it was, and I had to face my issues of deserving and get my self-esteem into shape.

The universal aspect of my story is that, when we marry we invest a lot of ourselves in bonding with our partner. Our unconscious expectation is to receive the loving behaviors we experienced with our parents, but even better love, healing love, because we have chosen our partner. Therefore, we expect our partner to know what we need and automatically give us that love in the way that we need it.

In that sense, we "parentify" our partners and assume they know all kinds of things about us that they do not. We want them to offer an unconditional love that is impossible. At some point, the reality of that expectation breaks down and we become aware that we are separate individuals and need to take responsibility for creating what we want.

I tell my story because it illustrates the feminine journey and how we choose a marriage partner that inevitably reopens our childhood wounds. I was so careful, I thought, to choose a God-centered man who would be loyal to me. In fact, Michael is totally honorable. His innocence sometimes frustrated me because he saw his life's path through meditation and his actions exemplified an altruism that did not allow me to feel important to him. Yes, he was innocent and honorable, but he was not loving and personal, and that was what I wanted from him. I eventually pressed him to break through the impersonal veneer of meditative spirituality.

## Completing Psyche's Three Tasks

When it came down to it, all I had to do was ask Michael to choose me and put me first. I told him I was happy to share him with God. God could come before me, but not meditation, and certainly not the meditation organization. He agreed. It was as simple as that. I had learned what I wanted and didn't want. I had defined my boundaries. I had learned how to deal with my feelings. Learning how to not act out of anger was a big step.

In the myth of Psyche, her sorting of the seeds symbolizes the defining of one's self, and understanding one's needs and desires. It symbolizes sorting out the possibilities of life. What are your dreams and which ones will you realize? Sorting things out and organizing your life is important, whether it is your house-hold, professional life, or relationships. A woman needs to know herself: how she feels, what she wants, what she values. Then she needs to gain skills through long practice, which enhances her abilities and enables her to achieve her goals. Fulfilling a woman's purpose in life requires attention to detail and systematically working on defined projects.

In my story, it took a long time for me to realize that I wanted our marriage and family to come first in Michael's life, before the meditation organization.

The years that followed Michael's pledge to shift his focus towards our marriage were still challenging while I learned how to manage myself when Michael wasn't talking to me, which is a behavior he used when he felt distant from me. This ties back to the symbolism of collecting the golden wool.

Collecting the golden wool from the divine rams alludes to learning how to address male anger indirectly, by allowing your husband to go to his cave and process his feelings. It symbolizes mastering the world of intense masculine emotions. The feminine personality can overcome male aggressiveness without confronting it. The wise woman waits for her husband to calm down and retire to his cave, and then she can go about her business. She leaves him there and knows she can get what she needs from him later.

In my contemporary version of the story, I learned to let Michael have his feelings and not assume that I was their ultimate cause. That meant I didn't need to react to him. I could let him have his space to sort himself out and understand himself at his own pace. I had to not assume that I was wrong in the situation, nor assume that Michael was right. I learned to stay centered and wait for Michael to come back and continue the conversation on his terms. I understood that Michael was as wounded as I was.

Collecting water from the River Styx symbolizes the deepening of your sense of self and realizing your connection to an unbounded source of life. The images of this part of the myth represent learning to move through the chaotic world of ideas and raging emotions in a productive way. The source of the River Styx, with its forbidding cliffs, fierce dragons, and poisonous vapors represents the unconscious, are filled with images that create chaotic emotions. The eagle represents a woman's power to learn how to rise above the situation, and swoop down and deal with one specific thing. The eagle did not make the approach to the source any easier for anyone else, but did complete a particular task. Using the goblet to collect a little bit of the waters of life is a metaphor for creating an ego structure out of the unbounded waters of life.

Women must develop a sense of their individual selves in order to become equal partners with their husbands. Nature, in the form of children and relationships in general, pushes women to adapt, nurture, and do whatever it takes to care for those relationships. Unfortunately, doing so can lead a woman to lose her own identity. When a woman rediscovers and values her sense of self, often in her thirties, she can define a more independent voice for feminine creativity and become a stronger kind of partner.

That is the growth of an independent identity and a connection to God. I was growing in self-esteem, internalizing a new respect from my professional accomplishments. I experienced the love and admiration of wise mentors who were catalysts for shaping my philosophy of life.

However you personalize these steps of development, the point here is that the ancients speak to us in metaphors that translate into modern psychological language. We continue to appreciate these stories because they contribute wisdom to the human family about what it means to be human and how one can develop one's self to the fullest.

# Chapter 10
# Creating Your Ideal Marriage

So what did I do to create a new marriage with the same husband? I began looking at myself as an individual with intrinsic value. That was part of an extraordinary experience at a pivotal time when, on the one hand, I was a chaplain on the receiving end of wise supervision, and on the other, learning to give love and understanding to strangers in great hardship, including the approach of death. Providing pastoral care to individuals in life's darkest moments taught me compassion in a new way. Opening my heart to others may have helped me experience this for myself.

When I confessed my darkest secrets of teenage misbehaviors to George Markum, my pastoral counselling supervisor, I sparked his memory of his days as a minister. The sweetest relief of loving acceptance swept through my mind and body as I released my greatest fears about my goodness. I felt returned to God's grace and love instantly, and knew the significance of that moment. I am forever grateful to George for his role in my life's journey. I had tried to resolve my issues intellectually and through meditation, but that had only hidden my shame and protected it with a wall of intelligent defensiveness.

I was now free to claim a more authentic self-esteem, a sense of personal value connected to a renewal of my personal integrity. Finding love and peace internally, I was able to grasp that "there is no love to get, only love to give." I now felt connected to a personal spiritual source. With this concept and new experience, I was able to detach from my neediness and dependence on relationships. If I were going to have a loving marriage, I would have to provide the love. That was a new point of view for me.

I was in my mid-thirties at the time, reading and going to many classes, searching for the principles that could empower my life. One of the principles asserted that life duplicates our thoughts about ourselves. So I decided to use my life as a laboratory for testing that principle. If I created a loving interaction with Michael, it would show me that my beliefs about myself and my life were truly positive for deserving and lovability. If I produced a conflict, then I would look inward to discover the underlying doubt or insecurity, and take responsibility for the breakdown in communication. I was constantly challenging myself to source my life with good energy to create a loving partnership. My mantra was: "There is no love to get, only love to give."

Those ideas did not exist in a vacuum. I had been a student of philosophy, psychology, and theology my entire thinking life, and had come to believe in the possibility of partnership with a God that is personal, powerful, and creative. I felt passionate about those ideas and I saw the quality of my life would depend on my taking responsibility for everything that happened in my relationship with Michael. I was applying the same principle in other areas of my life as well.

Those principles gave me the courage to hear Michael's anger and not take it personally. I saw how so many of his wounds did not begin with me, though my anger and criticisms poured salt into them. His silence for days on end was a learned behavior from childhood, when his mother withdrew in anger for long periods of time. I began to feel compassion for Michael, and see him as a good but wounded man, rather than as a controlling man. That gave me the strength and vision to support and coach him while he visited with his dying father.

My conversation with Michael started with my challenge to him. He was traveling to New York from California every other weekend. I felt he was spending meaningless time playing doctor with his dad. That caused me to lay down the gauntlet and define a boundary. "Make it meaningful and be a son," I said. But I saw he had no idea of what I was talking about, and so I coached him.

Michael often tells the story of his personal conversation with his father, its impact on his father's experience of dying, and on Michael's experience of personal relationship. His experiences leading up to his father's passing transformed him, and the outcome seemed miraculous: Michael never expected spiritual value from relationships, but then there it was. The power of love in his life overwhelmed him. The experience brought my husband back to me, integrated his personality, and made him a better man.

I could not have planned or predicted that outcome. My pure intention to tell my truth to Michael and support him caused the transformation. What happened was beyond any calculation. My coaching stimulated a loving conversation between Michael and his father that lifted his father's depression. It also changed his family dynamic by releasing the tension they felt with each other. I did not foresee how powerful Michael's goodbye with his father would be.

At the same time, my project to create an intimate marriage did not rely on that experience. Our day-to-day listening and loving were already creating a shift in our lives. Michael was learning how to tell me his thoughts and feelings, whatever they were, and I would not react. I would not be hurt. I could deal with life as it was. He was recovering from anger more quickly, and I was centered and okay. I think that helped him feel safe when he shared his feelings with me. We were working together and our trust grew.

You need boldness and humility to create love and take responsibility for everything in your marriage, and when you can find those qualities within you, the results can be transformative. You and your partner will not recreate the experience Michael and I have had, but yours can encompass just as much healing. Taking responsibility and creating love are a world away from feeling hopeless and dependent. But I traveled that distance to find those principles, practice them, and experience my own power to create good in my life.

Interventions by the supernatural creatures who counseled Psyche at each step of her journey helped her accomplish each task that Aphrodite set for her. I remember reading Psyche's story as a young woman and thinking, "She can't even accomplish these feats on her own. The story infantilizes her." I just didn't understand then as I do now. When you have a willingness to grow, and you stretch and lean into the next step of your development, teachers will show up in your life to guide you on your path. I have experienced this many times, and have seen it in others' lives as well. I have so many special guides to thank for my progress in life. They feel like intervention from a higher source. I am so grateful for the help they provided at each step of my journey.

Yes, this has been my journey. It required courage and perseverance, yet I developed new capabilities at each step. Just like Psyche, I sometimes felt lost, yet I kept pressing on. There was always a lighthouse in the form of some teacher with a key that unlocked the next door.

## *The Underworld Journey: Learning Focus, Intention and Control*

Gaining a stronger identity and purpose, and learning to create a loving relationship with Michael did not prepare me to deal with the loss of my dearest girlfriend, Betsy, when I was fifty years old. Her illness and death devastated me. I fell into a deep despair where life seemed pointless. I felt lost. All I saw about life was loss.

At that point, our daughters were in college and graduate school. Their absence from our home had surprised me with a sadness that magnified Betsy's illness and death. I buried myself in work, telling myself I should do this because it paid their tuition. Yet my days seemed rote and empty of their usual spark of purpose. Adding to that, Michael began a life transition with his work, ending his private practice in family medicine and deciding to retrain in a new but related field of rejuvenative and anti-aging medicine. That was difficult for me because Michael seemed vulnerable to forces in business and medicine, and I could not help him directly. I could only focus on my own work and trust Michael. Michael and I were very close during that ten-year period, but I had no idea of where our desires or his efforts would lead us. It was hard to see anything.

I now realize that Betsy's passing gave me an opportunity to understand that my bond with Michael was more important than how any of his projects turned out. It was an unusual generosity from me that I can only credit to a letting go that became possible because I appreciated the value of love in my life. Somehow, I was able to just love Michael and support him through his explorations and adventures, wrong turns, and corrections during that uncertain period, and still be okay.

During that time I felt very quiet. I was very focused on my work, my own tasks. In retrospect, I walked through my days like

Psyche walked through the underworld. My speech was controlled. I did not offer to be extraordinarily helpful outside my work, nor was I needy. I gave Michael lots of space, as I did my now married children. I felt centered, alone but not lonely. I was digesting many losses, and I had a lot to think about.

Betsy's death taught me more than the importance of love. She taught me that people aren't interchangeable. She was special. No new friend will ever replace who she is for me. Michael's preciousness to me became starkly apparent. I realized that he was more than a husband. He's this amazing and unique individual with whom I have the privilege of sharing my life. While I might be disappointed if he is unable to re-create a business, he means much more than that to me. That allowed me to move through those years in love and trust. I was with my precious friend and partner, Michael.

While the new business Michael eventually created exceeded his expectations and mine, the true miracle for me is how I let go of my fear and aligned myself with love and trust. It was a death of a part of my personality that I liken to Psyche's second crisis, her travel through the underworld culminating in her decision to open the box that contained Persephone's secret of feminine beauty, the ointment of the gods. There she died because of her bold desire to be Eros' lover, and came back to life through Eros's intervention as his equal and precious partner.

Psyche's journey to and from the underworld symbolizes a time in the life of a woman when she goes through a transformation that feels like a darkness, perhaps a mild depression, even while she learns fundamental lessons. The descent to the underworld represents a woman completing a phase of her journey where she integrates her growth as an independent woman. The journey to the underworld required all the individuation that Psyche accomplished, along with a willingness to surrender herself to her highest purpose and not submit to any emotional distractions. That self-discipline and perseverance allowed Psyche to feel herself worthy of partnership with Eros.

In Psyche's last phase of her journey, she saw herself disheveled and bruised. She wanted to regain her beauty to once again reunite with Eros. This symbolizes Psyche's intention to integrate the feminine qualities of beauty along with the inner strength she gained through accomplishing the four tasks. Dying and coming back to life represents a movement where the individual ego expands to a new sense of self. The story represents this by transforming Psyche into an eternal goddess, an equal with Eros.

How did I come back to life? I admit that was a puzzle to remember. The years of quietness were many. My first impulse was to say, "It just happened." On closer inspection, I see that Michael drew me out by his many invitations to meet him when his plane came back into town every week and have dinner at our favorite restaurant. When his new plans took form, he cajoled me into moving my practice into his office, in a different city.

We started taking dance lessons at a new level. Michael was enthusiastic about competing with me at a high level of ballroom dancing and going beyond the social dancing we had done for years. That has been a dream-come-true for me. He took leadership in writing our books by his vision for the book and making deadlines happen. He is the leader of our family by making sure we have schedules to visit the children who now have their own beautiful children.

My life is filled with creativity that has blossomed in every direction. Could it be that Michael has brought me back to life as Eros did for Psyche? I am willing to say so. It is a striking parallel and I can acknowledge him generously for the abundant life I live now as Michael's equal partner.

I find every nuance of the story of Psyche meaningful. I use her story to illustrate a sequence of steps in development that are precise and important in describing how a woman's life can unfold if she is willing to develop herself and pursue the growth of partnership with her husband. I want you to personalize the story in your own life, because I believe it illuminates the path so beautifully. This ancient myth asserts that marriage is developmentally important for your journey as a woman while many of the tasks that create important growth are independent projects.

My own life story took me along much of the path, as I am now in my sixties. Michael has noticed that I am softer. My focus is more on love and a deeper level of life experience. When I work with people, I can feel where they are in their lives and where they need to grow. It all comes quicker to me and more from the heart than ever. The intensity of love with Michael has increased. The experience of love and being loved has changed. Love has become concentrated and very personal.

## *Summary of the Journey*

In the first part of my journey to create the partnership I desired, I needed to develop my inner strength and gain confidence based on hard-won maturity. That included finding my own voice, discovering my true needs and desires, learning to deal effectively with male anger, and developing my own skills in life including creating firm boundaries in relationships.

All that was only half the story, however, approximating Psyche's first three tasks. The second part of my story involves Psyche's fourth task and includes my becoming centered and confident in my own competence and at the same time learning to trust and accept Michael as a distinct and separate personality. I found it paradoxical that by requesting behaviors while simultaneously accepting Michael's unique personality, he has been willing to stretch to make me happy. I have learned a sweet humility that I do not have all the answers. I am able to wait for answers and solutions that come from a bigger place than my personality.

Michael has been the home for my heart and soul on this earth. He has responded to my deepest wishes for love and understanding, and for the care of my children, parents, and friends. As much as I take care of him, he takes care of me, and maybe more. We think together, teach together, dance together, and adventure in all ways together. It has taken a lifetime to create this, and I am eternally grateful.

# Part 4

## Applying the Psycho-Spiritual Stages to Your Own Life

# Chapter 11

# Michael and Barbara's Story in Developmental Terms

Now we want to retell our stories in developmental stage terms to help you apply the stages to your own life.

Michael had a typical developmental pattern for a man. He moved away from his parents as a teen to attend college, and felt distant and disappointed in his parents because they were not sympathetic with his need to separate from the family. This was Michael's experience of the orphan stage.

Going to college for Michael meant independent thinking and the orphan and wanderer phases of searching for ideas and ideals to identify with. He then settled into family life when he married Barbara and started a family. Those, of course, are caretaker characteristics. His involvement with meditation was also a belonging experience in a community in which he received knowledge that he valued. This belonging stage ended when the demands of a medical career that included running a business and becoming a boss pushed him into the warrior stage in his early thirties.

Barbara also had the experience of growing distant from her parents and feeling disappointment in them. College allowed her to identify her interests and values. That was her wandering stage, filled with new ideas and ideals. Her willingness to adapt in her relationship to Michael and participate in the meditation community where she passively received knowledge are features of caretaker functioning. Received knowledge is a form of learning in which the learner does not critically reflect upon the knowledge, and so we consider it as traditional values or caretaking knowledge. Creating a home and raising two girls cemented her caretaking stage.

When Barbara went back to graduate school to complete her Ph.D., her daughters were five and seven. That put her in the tumultuous transition between caretaker and warrior. That created many conflicts in the marriage. Michael, as a warrior, felt Barbara was too concerned with family issues. From Barbara's perspective as a caretaker struggling toward warrior, Michael appeared distant.

Then, as Barbara transitioned to a warrior in her late thirties, she found her voice to express her needs, and sought new strategies for creating a good marriage. She also focused on her own career.

With Barbara's encouragement, Michael's growth in emotional intimacy with his father's passing and his reconciling with his mother pushed him into a stage of deeper compassion and love for others. This exemplified the beginning of the movement from warrior to wise elder. Fully developing that wisdom took many years to accomplish.

Barbara's movement toward wise elder also started from grief and loss. The loss of her best friend, Betsy, and her empty nest gave her a new perspective and an added softness. Her experiences, and her work as a counselor for individuals and couples, allowed her own personality to move to where greater wisdom could come through her individuality. With encouragement from Michael, Barbara began increasingly to express her creative impulse in the world of self-expression. This is seen in Michael's encouraging her to move her counseling practice into Michael's office where she became a co-director, owning her part of the ongoing marriage classes, writing this book on marriage, and engaging more intensely in competitive ballroom dancing.

Notice how the developmental stages show up over a lifetime. Equally important is the interplay of each partner's growth on the other that occurs for mutual benefit. Although the transitions between stages can be very uncomfortable, there is great value in holding on and growing through these periods. We believe in the potential of marriage between two committed partners to mature you, heal you and fulfill your potential as an integrated, individuated human being.

Notice how Barbara encouraged Michael to come from his heart which led to his experience of breaking out of the warrior phase and moving into the wise elder phase as seen in his experiences with his dad and his mom. As the Rebbe says: "The man will learn from his woman that he too can reach within others and provide nurture."

Notice how Michael encouraged Barbara to move her counseling practice to his new office, to conduct classes on marriage, to write this book on marriage and to intensely pursue competitive ballroom dancing. This supported Barbara to be creative in her world, self-expressed, and accomplished. As the Rebbe says: "and the woman will learn that she too can conquer."

We continue to enjoy a growing delight in our marriage. As two very independent, successful, career-oriented individuals, we come together in an increasingly more joyful appreciation of our differences, and a deepening of love and romance.

# Chapter 12
# Living the Hero's Journey

Stage changes are the trials of the hero's journey, which brings healing and development. Joseph Campbell describes the hero's journey in his groundbreaking book, *The Hero with a Thousand Faces*. In psychological language, one can express the adult phase of the journey in terms of the challenges of moving from caretaker to warrior, and from warrior to wise elder. Each stage change feels like a death, and has the symbolic analogies of falling into a deep well or into a whirlpool where all is lost. Watery symbolism usually represents the unconscious.

As you move from dwelling in a stage to letting go of its worldview, you may experience a descent into emptiness, depression, despair, and a fear of losing all. Many use such feelings as a reason to divorce. We counsel you to be conscious of the stage transitions and the hero's journey. Be aware of those transitions and do not mistake them for problems in your marriage.

You may find your spouse is supportive of your new direction, or he or she may be frightened. Big problems may occur if one partner is changing and moving through a stage transition and the other is not. We designed the sharing exercises in our workbook, *Falling In Love Forever*, to stimulate the growth of both partners. Sharing and accepting your partner's worldview is essential for your own development.

The world as you know it is going away. Willingly or unwillingly, you are moving into a new life. The death of a loved one, the loss of a job, or a crisis in a relationship are common paths that can take you unwillingly to a new stage. It could be that a new career or project consciously calls you, and you go willingly. Perhaps a book or conversation with new ideas pulls you toward a new way of being in the world.

## Two Predictable Crises in the Hero's Journey

Joseph Campbell described two phases of death or descents for the hero. In Psyche's story, she was bereft when Eros left her; she wanted to die. Later, when she completed her challenges and opened the box containing the beauty ointment of the gods, she actually did die, and Eros revived her. Likewise, Percival was devastated and depressed for years after he failed in his first attempt to reach the Grail. Then, just before his second entry into Grail Castle, he fought the foreign knight in the battle in which his sword broke. Percival was at the mercy of the foreign knight, when the knight granted Percival mercy and then revealed himself to be Percival's half-brother. Percival thus learned the lessons of defeat and humility.

In both stories, the first descent is the transition from caretaker to warrior, which takes the protagonists away from the comfort of belonging to their quests to pursue their purpose and ideals. Michael's movement from caretaker to warrior began when his meditation teacher sent him home from Switzerland to fulfill his vocation. For Barbara, the pressure to individuate came from the recognition that her dependence on her marriage for happiness was not working, and that she needed to become more than her relationship.

The second descent involves moving from warrior to wise elder, from identifying with our beliefs and ideals to letting go of the ego sense of self and becoming more compassionate, accepting, and inspired by wisdom. For Michael, the second descent encompassed the period of the passing of both his parents as a learning experience about feelings and an elevated appreciation of the unique individuals in his life. For Barbara, the passing of her best friend, Betsy, and the departure of her daughters from home created a new perspective about time and the purpose of life. It enabled her to more deeply accept life as it is and grow in compassion for others.

Our stage transitions were slow; it took us years to consolidate the changes. We needed help from mentors and supportive friends, and appreciate, in retrospect, the challenges posed by our "enemies." Each transition ended with a rebirth to a new level of life with new skills, new tools, and keys to unlock our worlds.

Do not blame your spouse for your life challenges. They are a part of the hero's journey. The ultimate developmental destination is a very deep quality of love and appreciation of others. The quality of love in the caretaker stage is belonging to the group or family. In the warrior stage, you love from your principles and beliefs as the foundation of relationship. In the wise elder stage, you love as an individual. You appreciate the various beliefs and principles of others in your life. You understand how differences in people fit into a bigger picture of the wholeness of life.

As a wise elder, you appreciate each person in your life as a wondrous individual who is on a journey. You enjoy them and feel compassion for the drama in their life. You love them as you see deeply into their soul while you accept them as a magnificent person on their path. Your actions with people are helpful and caring.

# Chapter 13

# How Differences in Individual Growth Affect Marriage

A complete analysis of the ramifications of two individuals in a marriage, and the interaction of their developmental trajectories, would require a book in itself. And although we may take on that project eventually, we regret that it is not possible to do it here. We have, however, some practical insights and applications that you can use right now. They involve critical developmental junctures in marriage.

## *Orphan Adult in Marriage*

Most married adults are at least in the caretaker stage, where both partners have a great desire to form a relationship and build a family. There are, however, some orphan adults who are married, and they fulfill some of the caretaker role. For example, they may have a job or be responsible financially. They know it is time to be married. But they are really just teenagers in adult bodies, and not able to maintain a relationship by being responsible to another person.

Issues that often inhibit the development of orphans are the use of recreational drugs or indulging in other addictions, a history of abuse or neglect as a child, or other serious psychological imbalances. While they expect their partner to be trustworthy, they frequently care only for their own needs and are not trustworthy in return. They don't understand the rules for creating a marriage. If they want a good marriage, they need to understand and resolve the source of their anxieties. For addicts and abused children, the anxiety usually comes from some form of shame. They need to bring their addiction under control and/or bring their psychological development up to their chronological age.

Orphan adults need to learn how to keep their word, tell the truth, make amends, and forgive. That is the bridge that allows relationships to develop to the mutuality of the caretaker stage. Orphans are unable to maintain adult relationships. They have buddies. The influence of a healthy spiritual life, twelve-step programs, and individual psychotherapy can facilitate their transitions. It is difficult to be married to an orphan partner, and if both partners are orphans, the marriage is highly unstable.

Students who go to college often gravitate away from traditions of family, religion, and patriotism and begin a wandering stage in which they define their values. Most young adults come back to family and tradition, but on new terms as they create their own families and become caretakers. They may choose to belong to groups or organizations with whom they identify.

If a young adult continues to live with his or her parents after college, the young adult's personal development may be stunted. Independent living involving taking responsibility for finances as well as creating social relationships and a possible romantic partnership propels young persons to stretch and grow in maturity. Young adults who live with their parents may not have access to this stimulation for development and their progress in life can be delayed. Pathways to caretaker and warrior may not be available to a dependent in the parents' home.

## Caretaker Marriage

The caretaker stage is a very comfortable place for married life. Individuals in this stage value the nurturing of family. Many of us marry when we are caretakers if we married young. Persons in this stage are capable of collaboration and self-sacrifice in a relationship in which belonging and mutuality of feeling are key values. In fact, relationships are so important in this stage that one's significant relationships define the self.

The school of developmental psychology that focuses on "structural development" maintains that a caretaker partner dwells in the world of interpersonal relationships. Fish are not aware that water surrounds them, as water surrounds everything in their universe. In a similar way, orphans dwell in their needs and desires. Transitioning from one stage to the next involves stepping out of one's dwelling. In the case of going from caretaker to warrior, partners begin to experience themselves as separate from their marriages. Warriors typically have a richer intellectual life than caretakers, and so develop finer abilities to negotiate the needs of their marriages. They make their decisions more on the basis of principle and less on feeling, in contrast to when they were caretakers.

## Caretaker-Warrior Marriage

Development-oriented therapists know that individuals are starting to transition to the warrior stage when their conversations include issues of resentment about what has been sacrificed for their relationships, and issues of guilt for wanting things for themselves. Such conflicts brew until they are resolved in favor of a self that is comfortable identifying and asserting individual values and limits. Warriors are generally more defined and individuated persons, but can be less acquiescing partners. They are able to operate in a marriage with many more skills because their identity is no longer the relationship.

A young adult may marry and, as a domestic partner, create a family and provide the nurturing environment of family life that is representative of the caretaker. Family life is not an individualistic endeavor, especially when there are children. This can put the domestic partner at a developmentally different place than the workplace partner. It all depends on whether the workplace partner has a challenging and stimulating job. If the job is not challenging, the two caretaker partners can have a comfortable balance and share the same values over a prolonged period of time.

If the workplace partner is seriously committed to his or her profession, striving for goals that require a high degree of responsibility and competence, the workplace partner will inevitably attain the warrior level. The differences between caretaker and warrior can be workable for a couple who define their roles in a traditional manner or for partners who accept the reversal of traditional roles.

Such an arrangement can be comfortable for years and then unexpectedly explode into uncomfortable tension when the caretaker partner transitions to warrior. Most women make that transition in their mid to late 30s. When it occurs later, there is usually an even greater upheaval. Partners who are caretakers make significant contributions to family and community. Developmental psychologists emphasize that later stages do not necessarily signify a higher standard of person. Caretakers are the good citizens who are the backbone of society. Family life can suffer when caretaker individuals enter the warrior stage if the family still needs their nurture.

The caretaker partner can be devoted and nurturing, which can work well for a long while. The warrior partner will be a natural leader, and create a sense of direction and safety for the couple. In time, however, the caretaker partner often comes to interpret a warrior spouse as self-centered, distant, or controlling. The warrior spouse has a more defined self, so the caretaker partner is not wrong in his or her perception, though an important misunderstanding occurs. Yes, they miss the connection they used to have. They used to live in the implicit connectedness of caretaker values. But the warrior partner now lives more in autonomous thinking and is not as interested in empathy. The combination of individuation with empathy will come later, if and when they become wise elders.

The relationship is not easy for the warrior partner, either. The caretaker spouse appears loyal and caring, but often boring to the warrior partner. The caretaker partner is typically very bonding oriented and thinks mostly about practical matters, not ideas or self-reflection. Conversation, then, between caretaker and warrior spouses lags during this period.

Caretaker and warrior differences in a marriage can be a risky time for a marriage if the partners do not understand what is going on. Learning the practices we teach of sharing, reflecting, and analyzing the dynamics of a relationship is a warrior function. That is what helps partners in different stages connect better with each other. Over time, the caretaker spouse comes up to the level of warrior, exerting a softening influence on the warrior spouse by promoting empathy in the couple's experience.

Husbands and wives must appreciate each other in their different gender experiences and in their unique experiences as individuals. The practices in our workbook, *Falling In Love Forever*, allow each partner to clarify and distinguish his or her own needs and desires along with those of the partner. That helps each partner to individuate, mature, and develop his or her sense of self. Practicing the communication of feelings and thoughts also encourages growth through each stage. From there they can build a warrior-warrior relationship in which each is conscious of working on the relationship, as each no longer dwells in relationship.

## *Warrior Marriage*

Warrior couples can benefit from our instruction, too, because warriors, while reflective and articulate, can lack empathy. Such a couple has the potential of sounding like two lawyers negotiating because they are clear about their point of view and where they define their boundaries. Our exercises help them soften, share feelings, and grow closer.

The changes in our lives can seem mysterious. Structural stage development explains the ebb and flow of our attachments to those we love. Understanding this and learning ways to stimulate stage development will help prevent broken marriages. As couples recognize the patterns of their relationships, it becomes much easier to diffuse tensions and support each other's growth. This knowledge can be a huge relief for spouses who have misunderstood their partner or even misinterpreted themselves. It makes us happy to see couples understand each other, and relax and enjoy their deep bond as they travel together through life.

# Chapter 14

# Seeing Your Own Life Stages

Now let's look at the different stages and transitions of your life as you alternated between attachment and autonomy, starting from your family of origin and continuing through your adult life. In the Time Period column, enter your age at the time you were in each stage. In the Experiences column, enter your experiences in more detail. What was going on then? What major life events were happening? (For example: college, first job, marriage, moved away from parents, started a business, etc.)

Remember, the reason you are looking at these stages is to understand how you moved through them on your journey, and how each stage affected your experience of relationship. Notice how your feelings and perceptions of marriage changed from one stage to another. Your marriage stimulates your and your spouse's process of partnered growth and movement through the stages, but it is also an independent process that deeply affects each of you individually. The feelings of distance and closeness are inevitable as you move through life. We want you to understand each other's growth and development so that you can support each other and stay connected.

Complete the following chart, and see how it applies to your relationship challenges. Share what you find with your partner.

| Stage | Time Period | Experiences and Events |
|---|---|---|
| **1. Innocent** | | Feeling close with family of origin |
| **2. Orphan** | | Feeling distant from family of origin |
| **2.5. Wanderer** | | Exploring new ideas and different ways of belonging |
| **3. Caretaker** | | Feeling close and creating a family for belonging |
| **3.5. Transition from Caretaker to Warrior** | | Feeling conflicted between belonging and need for independence |

| Stage | Time Period | Experiences and Events |
|---|---|---|
| **4. Warrior** | | Feeling committed to ideals and independence and somewhat distant from partner |
| **4.5. Transition from Warrior to Wise Elder** | | Feeling sadness, loss of purpose, lack of enthusiasm, boredom |
| **5. Wise Elder** | | Feeling close to loved ones and self is more transparent |

Looking at development in this way is a very sophisticated lens through which to view life's journey. It is not an ordinary psychosocial description of personal growth, in which you grow through life stages because you age into the stage automatically. This is different. Structural stage theory accounts for qualitative changes in an individual's way of thinking and relating, and there is no guarantee that an individual will progress beyond orphan or caretaker without a significant internal or external stimulus.

Talking about structural stage theory in the same conversation with clinical applications for improving marital satisfaction brings together two communities that have not really become acquainted yet. Further, talking about structural stage theory is difficult because it is a very abstract field.

In our classes, we talk about how the transition that women make from caretaker to warrior typically occurs later for them than for their husbands. An exception might be a woman who has focused on career and begins married life in her thirties. It is a rare woman who does not know what we are talking about. Most women nod their heads in silent or vocal appreciation when we refer to the anger that rages within from all the accommodating they have done, and how much they want and need to change.

We also discuss the corresponding need that most men have to learn compassion for their wives as their wives find themselves and learn to ask for what they want. We have geared the skills we teach, and those outlined in our workbook, *Falling In Love Forever*, to the developmental enrichments that partners need to incorporate into their behavioral toolbox, self-understanding, and remapping of their marriage.

Many psychological models have antecedents in ancient literature. The next and final chapter describes a literary metaphor from the Talmud, an ancient Jewish text from 400 AD, which elucidates the stages of growth of a marriage over a lifetime.

# Chapter 15

# The Stages of Marriage

The Talmud describes the stages of marriage in a parable that we elaborate on in this final chapter. You have already learned about the dynamics of stage development for each partner in marriage, but you can also use the lens of developmental stages to look at the qualities of a marriage. The character of a marriage represents the development of its partners. We have found this perspective to be helpful because it displays how differences in the partners' development create different kinds of marriages.

Marriages go through stages of development just like individuals, and a model such as we present here allows couples to see how a conscious married life can evolve. We hope this motivates you and invites you to reflect on the stages of your marriage as you read our interpretation of the ancient parable: "A man who dreams of a river or kettle or a bird can look forward to peace."

## *The River*

According to the parable, the first stage of marriage is like living across a river. In the beginning of married life, your skills revolve around trading and negotiating in order to get what you want. The partners are like two communities living across a river from each other. You share and trade with each other. You become familiar with what the other likes and dislikes. You learn to cooperate in ways that benefit both parties.

In marriage, you are a separate entity looking to create a greater good for yourself. The river stage of married life corresponds to individuals living in the orphan and beginning of the caretaker stages. Think of your marriage when you were in your twenties and just getting to know each other. That is usually the river stage of relationship. Newly married couples who are older usually spend less time in this stage.

## The Kettle

The next stage of married life is like a kettle containing cold water and raw grain. As fire heats the kettle, the heat from the fire causes the cold water and raw grain to combine and create a new entity: cooked grain. The fire and water represent the male and female qualities, respectively. Water alone would ruin the grain by allowing rot to spoil it. Fire alone would destroy it by burning. But by working together with an intentional focus, a new product emerges out of the heat and the cold, a product that would not have been possible with just one or the other.

Marriage partners' progress to a stage where they can create opportunities and possibilities that would not be available on their own. They work together as a unit to create family life, which transcends what a lone individual could create. They no longer work as separate units like traders across a river. Rather, they are intimately connected and work closely with each other.

Think of the time when your relationship moved to the stage of working together to create something new in your lives that was bigger than your individual selves. For example: building a strong family life though partnership, successfully raising children; creating a business; supporting a group or organization that you both deeply believed in; or perhaps doing other creative projects together.

That is the beginning of intimate marriage, because the husband and wife must learn to work together. They need to appreciate each other, and be willing to collaborate and raise their family together. The husband learns to appreciate the feminine values of nurturing and connecting, and he incorporates those values into his personality. The wife learns to appreciate and incorporate the masculine values of independence and mastery. Both skill sets are essential to developing their marriage, raising their children, and providing for the family. The kettle stage of married life corresponds to individuals living in the caretaker stage and moving into the warrior stage.

The ancient story outlines the important learning that must take place in the kettle stage. We find a lot of emotional work and cognitive stretching occurs for partners who are moving from caretakers to warriors. There is tremendous pressure on couples to grow because of the new responsibilities and challenges that they face at this time. They need to master many skills and learn to work together.

The metaphor of the kettle recalls the image of fire and heat of the crucible that is critical to this process of learning to work together, understanding each other and creating enduring love.

## *The Bird*

The most sublime stage of married life is the bird stage. A bird can walk on the earth and fly in the heavens. Unlike the kettle stage, where the fire and water combine to create something new, the bird contains the two qualities within itself, integrating them into one being.

In addition, the bird has two wings and two feet to move through the realms of heaven and earth. Those limbs represent  the two individuals who are intimately connected and, through love, merge into one living being. Each of the individuals is living in a high stage of development, reflecting the highest level of marriage, in which the two individuals no longer function as separate entities in the relationship. The bird stage of married life corresponds to individuals who have moved from warriors to wise elders.

The symbolism of the bird suggests the intense experience of intimacy with each other. Common thoughts and desires arise naturally as if they came from one being, always thinking of the good of the other as much as of the good for themselves. When one has a desire, the other rushes to fulfill it. The minds and hearts of the couple become one. The metaphor of the bird suggests that a husband and wife have transformed their romantic relationship from a crucible for healing their deepest childhood wounds to a holy relationship that awakens the highest levels of the presence of God. Such a transformation is possible because they meet as equals, sharing trust and emotional acceptance of each other.

## Imagining a Precious Love

Imagine the possibility of married life created by a deep appreciation of your partner. That would allow you to fall in love with life itself and all the beauty present in life. Such a process requires both partners to mature deeply and develop in wisdom.

Perhaps that description of spiritual marriage is difficult for you to imagine. If so, think instead of falling in love with a character from one of your favorite movies. While watching the film, you have a depth of passion for the character on the screen, but you don't lose yourself in the process. You know that you're watching a movie, yet the character expands your heart. The character feels his or her joys and pains deeply, and you allow the character to transport you intensely on the movie's emotional roller coaster precisely because it is only a movie.

Because you deeply appreciate the movie, you do not wish to change or improve your favorite character. Rather, you just appreciate this character for who they are and the qualities they express. You love their good qualities and their shortcomings. You love the way they deal with the challenges the narrative presents. This quality of deeply loving but having no desire to improve the character you love is a characteristic of the love you experience when you live in the bird stage of marriage. This is the purest kind of love: loving for no reason. Just being present to your partner's essential nature and valuing your partner is fulfilling enough. (Of course, loving your actual husband or wife offers dimensions of intensity greater than enjoying a movie character and your movie of life has not ended, as you are continuing to live it.)

You can further imagine developing a deep appreciation for the great artistry of the writer and director of the movie, who expanded your heart by creating your favorite character. That developed quality of love for the artistic creator is a parallel for a true appreciation of God's creation. Appreciation of God's creation is a big step toward a mature falling in love with God.

Romantic, passionate love requires that you maintain mystery, adventure, and novelty. It requires that you do not pretend to know all the aspects of your lover. While you perceive so much depth in your partner, you can begin to see that you cannot possibly understand all the dimensions of your partner's self. This perspective allows you to stay passionately in love with your partner. At the same time, your own self is free of possessiveness and neediness. That would turn off your partner's passion for you. As in the movie analogy, you are separate from your partner, but you fall in love with him or her over and over without neediness or possession.

The quality of love in the bird stage keeps romantic passion alive and vibrant. Passionate love in a long-term marriage is nurtured by feeling joy when you reconnect after being apart, attraction when you see your partner expressing his or her purpose for being on earth, and enjoying adventure and journey together. That occurs most fully in the bird stage of marriage.

Wise elder love brings great humility as you feel privileged to experience intense, unconditional love flowing through your life. At the same time, this love, in the form of compassion, creates great strength as your individual personality becomes open to greater dimensions of wisdom. As time goes on, that leads to the experience of falling in love with life itself.

## The Path of Transformation

The process of transformation from a river relationship to a kettle relationship to a bird relationship involves expanding the levels of acceptance of your partner and yourself. By dissolving your old hurts and fears, you create deeper levels of appreciation for your partner. As we have described in our personal stories, the dissolving of emotional wounds is a process that requires courage, commitment, and a vision of possibilities for your life. We have described the levels of personal and relationship growth, and shared the process we have experienced to help you through the crucible of your own romantic marriage.

# Conclusion

A self is much more attractive than a non-self. Each partner in a marriage will go on his or her own journey to develop an individual self through the developmental map we described. When each spouse feels that their journey is supported by their partner, the marriage will flower into a lifelong passionate romance.

Life itself will bring up issues and challenges. When life brings you to a stage transition, we want your awareness of stage changes to be a context for understanding what may be occurring in your life. The process of growth in marriage will not always be comfortable, particularly during stage transitions of one or both partners. Marriage is a process that is either growing or falling into distance and indifference. Marriage does not stay the same. It is not okay to be just okay. Coasting implies a winding down of energy.

In marriage, we may initially feel closeness, and later we may differentiate and become individuals again. It takes many skills to balance one's individuality with connection to a partner. Add children to the mix, and the relationship can get even more intense. Parenting our own children reminds us of what we received and didn't receive from our parents. Children also create dynamics that bring us together as a couple but also separate us if we are not working together as partners.

The patterns involve more individuality from the very beginning of the marriage when both partners are engaged in serious vocations. That could mean that conflict will come sooner. In some way or another, you must face your past abandonment or entrapment wounds and define what you want on a deeper level and hear your partner's needs as well. By doing so, you exercise your power to choose the quality of your relationship. Marriage cannot thrive without each partner taking his or her individual life seriously and consciously developing it.

We understand that a woman's life path is not exactly the same as a man's path, especially when you are in a marriage. While we understand the gender patterns we have described are not universally true, our intention is to support your individual development along with your evolution in the relationship.

We see marriage as an ordeal that is potentially transforming. It is a healing journey for each partner. Whether it transforms your life is up to you. There are many wisdom stories and mentors to help you on your way, but the inner work is a choice that only *you* can make.

And if you do, we wish you a joyous and successful journey.

# Epilogue

We want every man and woman out there to experience great love, and we feel strongly that there is no excuse not to. There are a finite number of skills you need to learn in order to have great love—all you need is the willingness to learn. We encourage you to learn these practical skills needed to navigate through the inevitable changes of your romantic partnership by reading our companion book, *Falling in Love Forever* and by taking our classes in person or online. In our course, we not only give you the tools, but we model them for you so that you are fully equipped to apply them for immediate results. You are not alone in the struggle to have a good marriage. We promise to teach you strategies you will use your whole life to allow you to fall in love forever with your current romantic partner.

Your marriage needs to be your number one priority. Do not let busyness be an excuse for letting your marriage slip into mediocrity. Invest in yourself and your marriage and learn the skills for *falling in love forever* with your current partner. Our classes are designed to protect your privacy so you do not share personal information with anyone but your partner.

Go to our website www.TheMarriageMap.com and enroll in our classes and get access to additional resources and materials.

## What our course participants are saying:

"Thank you for all your knowledge and assistance. It came at a time I felt all was lost." ~ Gabrielle C.

"I now have the ability to stop conflict on a dime. When conflict arises, we are able to move through it really quickly and maintain our connection instead of having it spiral into something bigger. The course has given us concrete skills we can apply immediately." ~ Kelsey

"This class saved our marriage! I cannot believe just four weeks ago we were on the road to divorce! I am so pleased and happy that The Good Lord guided us here!" ~ Shannon P.

"It's brought a new level of conversation that pretty much always leaves me feeling confident and very comfortable afterwards. There was always the sense of not knowing whether or not you were heard or understood before we took the course. Now there's the sense of understanding—there's no static. This is something I'm really glad we got into." ~ Nathan

"We received tools to see each other's point of view and to see a whole other level to our partner." ~ Shelly H.

"The course truly made us put our marriage at the forefront, at the very center of our life's radar screen and thus makes us more connected emotionally." ~ Rosie T.

# Bibliography

Campbell, J. *The Hero with a Thousand Faces.* Second Edition. New Jersey: Princeton University Press, 1949.

Cole-Whittaker, T. *What You Think of Me Is None of My Business.* New York: Putnam, 1979.

De Rougemont, D. *Love in the Western World.* New Jersey: Princeton University Press, 1983.

Feldman, A. *The River, the Kettle and the Bird.* New York: Feldheim, 1987.

Hendrix, H. *Getting the Love You Want.* New York: Henry Holt, 1988.

Hesse, H. *Narcissus and Goldmund.* New York: Bantam, 1968.

———. *Siddhartha.* New York: Farrar Straus and Giroux, 1968.

Jampolsky, G. *Love Is Letting Go of Fear.* Berkeley, Calif.: Celestial Arts, 1979.

Kegan, R. *The Evolving Self: Problem and Process in Human Development.* Cambridge, Mass,: Harvard University Press, 1982.

Napier, A., with Whitaker, C. *The Family Crucible.* New York: Harper & Row, 1978.

Osbon, D. (Ed.). *A Joseph Campbell Companion. Reflections on the Art of Living.* New York: HarperCollins, 1991.

Pearson, C. *The Hero Within: Six Archetypes We Live By.* San Francisco, Calif.: HarperCollins, 1998.

Pearson, C. *Awakening the Heroes Within: 12 Archetypes to Help Us Find Ourselves and Transform Our World.* New York: HarperCollins, 1991.

Small, J. *Psyche's Seeds.* New York: Putnam, 2001.

# About the Authors

# Barbara Grossman, Ph.D.

Dr. Barbara's background is in psychology and theology. She majored in philosophy and psychology at New York University, completed her Masters in Religion at Columbia University in 1975, and holds a Ph.D. in theology and counseling from The Claremont School of Theology since 1991. She is licensed as an individual, marriage, and family therapist. Her training included pastoral counseling with ministers who were cross-training in individual psychotherapy and marriage and family counseling. In addition, she worked with psychologists and psychiatrists in hospital and group practice settings.

Dr. Barbara's background integrates spiritual and psychological perspectives. This integration offers a special contribution for maturing individuals and couples. She deliberately chose the marriage, family, and child counselor's license because it represents a respect for the value of relationships in mental health and a desire to serve the purpose of creating good relationships. For the past 32 years, Dr. Barbara has maintained a busy private practice.

# Michael Grossman, M.D.

Dr. Michael is a board-certified family physician and a fellow of the American Academy of Anti-Aging Medicine. He has practiced since 1978 in nutritional and preventive medicine and has treated thousands of patients with an integrated holistic approach. Since 2003, Dr. Grossman has incorporated the latest technological advances into his practice of medicine, including laser skin rejuvenation and nonsurgical face lifts.

Since 2009, he has been specializing in anti-aging and regenerative medicine using bio-identical hormone replacement to assist men and women to reverse the effects of aging on their emotional and physical well-being. In 2014, Dr. Michael began using stem cell investigational protocols for a wide variety of degenerative diseases. In addition, Dr. Michael is an expert in treating male and female sexual dysfunction with stem cells and platelet rich plasma (o-shot and p-shot), as well as with Gainswave acoustic sound wave therapy.

Dr. Michael is a graduate of New York University School of Medicine. He was an Assistant Clinical Professor at the University of California at Irvine, School of Medicine from 2001 to 2008, where he trained medical students and residents in natural approaches that complement traditional medicine. Dr. Michael is also an active member of the fellowship in Anti-Aging and Regenerative Medicine.

Dr. Michael is the author of *The Vitality Connection: Ten Practical Ways to Optimize Health and Reverse the Aging Process* and lectures extensively on various topics of wellness, including stress reduction, nutrition, and reversing aging. He is also the author of *The Magic of Stem Cells: Activating Your Own Healing Power*.

Board Certifications, Associations and Training:

- Member of BodyLogicMD, a national network of highly trained physicians specializing in Natural Bioidentical Hormone Therapy.
- Fellow of the American Academy for Anti-Aging Medicine
- Extensive training in anti-aging provided by the Fellowship in Anti-Aging and Regenerative Medicine
- Affiliate Physician of the Cell Surgical Network

# Michael and Barbara Working Together

Drs. Michael and Barbara also facilitated weekly attitudinal healing classes from 1985 to 1997. These classes taught patients to use spiritual principles, attitudes, and beliefs that promote wellness through forgiveness and healing of resentments. In addition, for more than 30 years, Dr. Michael has taught thousands of people meditation and how to integrate spiritual experience into everyday life in weekly classes.

Since 1990, Drs. Michael and Barbara have been teaching a course called *Falling in Love Forever*. These relationship classes teach practical skills to allow couples to experience a profound deepening of love through the romantic process of life.

Dr. Michael is also a student of Kabbalah. Integrating Attitudinal Healing and Jewish spirituality has led Dr. Michael to teach bi-weekly classes in Kabbalah and Meditation in Orange County, California since 1986.

Michael and Barbara are amateur competitive ballroom dancers and have two married daughters and seven grandchildren.

You can contact Barbara and Michael through their web sites: **www.OCWellness.com** and **OCWellnessStemCell.com**.

For information about relationship classes contact them at: **www.TheMarriageMap.com.**